ACTIONS AND REACTIONS

RUDYARD KIPLING

The Centenary Edition

ACTIONS

AND

REACTIONS

BY

RUDYARD KIPLING

M

ISBN (cased) 0 333 32781 0
ISBN (paper) 0 333 32782 9

MACMILLAN LONDON LIMITED
London and Basingstoke

Associated companies in Auckland, Dallas,
Delhi, Dublin, Hong Kong, Johannesburg,
Lagos, Manzini, Melbourne, Nairobi,
New York, Singapore, Tokyo, Washington
and Zaria

First edition 1909
Reprinted 1909, 1910, 1917, 1927, 1936
Edition de Luxe 1909
Uniform edition 1909
Pocket edition 1909
Bombay edition 1914
Sussex edition 1937
Library edition 1951
Centenary edition 1968
Centenary edition (n.s.) 1982
Paperback edition 1983

Printed in Great Britain by
St. Edmundsbury Press
Bury St. Edmunds, Suffolk

CONTENTS

An Habitation Enforced

An Habitation Enforced

My friend, if cause doth wrest thee,
Ere folly hath much oppressed thee,
Far from acquaintance kest thee
Where country may digest thee . . .
Thank God that so hath blessed thee,
And sit down, Robin, and rest thee.
THOMAS TUSSER.

IT came without warning, at the very hour his
hand was outstretched to crumple the Holtz and
Gunsberg Combine. The New York doctors
called it overwork, and he lay in a darkened room,
one ankle crossed above the other, tongue pressed
into palate, wondering whether the next brain-
surge of prickly fires would drive his soul from
all anchorages. At last they gave judgment.
With care he might in two years return to the
arena, but for the present he must go across the
water and do no work whatever. He accepted
the terms. It was capitulation; but the Combine that had shivered beneath his knife gave him
all the honours of war. Gunsberg himself, full
of condolences, came to the steamer and filled
the Chapins' suite of cabins with overwhelming
flower-works.

3

'Smilax,' said George Chapin when he saw them. 'Fitz is right. I'm dead; only I don't see why he left out the "In Memoriam" on the ribbons!'

'Nonsense!' his wife answered, and poured him his tincture. 'You'll be back before you can think.'

He looked at himself in the mirror, surprised that his face had not been branded by the hells of the past three months. The noise of the decks worried him, and he lay down, his tongue only a little pressed against his palate.

An hour later he said: 'Sophie, I feel sorry about taking you away from everything like this. I—I suppose we're the two loneliest people on God's earth to-night.'

Said Sophie his wife, and kissed him: 'Isn't it something to you that we're going together?'

They drifted about Europe for months— sometimes alone, sometimes with chance-met gipsies of their own land. From the North Cape to the Blue Grotto at Capri they wandered, because the next steamer headed that way, or because some one had set them on the road. The doctors had warned Sophie that Chapin was not to take interest even in other men's interests; but a familiar sensation at the back of the neck after one hour's keen talk with a Nauheimed railway magnate saved her any trouble. He nearly wept.

'And I'm over thirty,' he cried. 'With all I meant to do!'

'Let's call it a honeymoon,' said Sophie. 'D'you know, in all the six years we've been married, you've never told me what you meant to do with your life?'

'With my life? What's the use? It's finished now.' Sophie looked up quickly from the Bay of Naples. 'As far as my business goes, I shall have to live on my rents like that architect at San Moritz.'

'You'll get better if you don't worry; and even if it takes time, there are worse things than —— How much have you?'

'Between four and five million. But it isn't the money. You know it isn't. It's the principle. How could you respect me? You never did, the first year after we married, till I went to work like the others. Our tradition and upbringing are against it. We can't accept *those* ideals.'

'Well, I suppose I married you for some sort of ideal,' she answered, and they returned to their forty-third hotel.

In England they missed the alien tongues of Continental streets that reminded them of their own polyglot cities. In England all men spoke one tongue, speciously like American to the ear, but on cross-examination unintelligible.

'Ah, but you have not seen England,' said a lady with iron-grey hair. They had met her in Vienna, Bayreuth, and Florence, and were grateful to find her again at Claridge's, for she commanded situations, and knew where prescriptions are most carefully made up. 'You ought to take an interest in the home of our ancestors—as I do.'

'I've tried for a week, Mrs. Shonts,' said Sophie, 'but I never get any further than tipping German waiters.'

'These are not the true type,' Mrs. Shonts went on. 'I know where you should go.'

Chapin pricked up his ears, anxious to run anywhere from the streets on which quick men something of his kidney did the business denied to him.

'We hear and we obey, Mrs. Shonts,' said Sophie, feeling his unrest as he drank the loathed British tea.

Mrs. Shonts smiled, and took them in hand. She wrote widely and telegraphed far on their behalf, till, armed with her letter of introduction, she drove them into that wilderness which is reached from an ash-barrel of a station called Charing Cross. They were to go to Rocketts—the farm of one Cloke, in the southern counties—where, she assured them, they would meet the genuine England of folklore and song.

Rocketts they found after some hours, four miles from a station, and, so far as they could judge in the bumpy darkness, twice as many from a road. Trees, kine, and the outlines of barns showed shadowy about them when they alighted, and Mr. and Mrs. Cloke, at the open door of a deep stone-floored kitchen, made them slowly welcome. They lay in an attic beneath a wavy, whitewashed ceiling, and because it rained, a

wood fire was made in an iron basket on a brick
hearth, and they fell asleep to the chirping of mice
and the whimper of flames.

When they woke it was a fair day, full of the
noises of birds, the smell of box, lavender, and
fried bacon, mixed with an elemental smell they
had never met before.

'This,' said Sophie, nearly pushing out the
thin casement in an attempt to see round the
corner, 'is—what did the hack——cabman say
to the railway porter about my trunk—" quite on
the top "? '

'No; " a little bit of all right." I feel
further away from anywhere than I've ever felt
in my life. We must find out where the telegraph office is.'

'Who cares?' said Sophie, wandering about,
hair-brush in hand, to admire the illustrated
weekly pictures pasted on door and cupboard.

But there was no rest for the alien soul till he
had made sure of the telegraph office. He asked
the Clokes' daughter, laying breakfast, while
Sophie plunged her face in the lavender bush
outside the low window.

'Go to the stile a-top o' the Barn field,' said
Mary, ' and look across Pardons to the next spire.
It's directly under. You can't miss it—not if
you keep to the footpath. My sister's the telegraphist there. But you're in the three-mile
radius, sir. The boy delivers telegrams directly
to this door from Pardons village.'

'One has to take a good deal on trust in this
country,' he murmured.

Sophie looked at the close turf, scarred only with last night's wheels; at two ruts which wound round a rickyard; and at the circle of still orchard about the half-timbered house.

'What's the matter with it?' she said. 'Telegrams delivered to the Vale of Avalon, of course,' and she beckoned in an earnest-eyed hound of engaging manners and no engagements, who answered, at times, to the name of Rambler. He led them, after breakfast, to the rise behind the house where the stile stood against the skyline, and, 'I wonder what we shall find now,' said Sophie, frankly prancing with joy on the grass.

It was a slope of gap-hedged fields possessed to their centres by clumps of brambles. Gates were not, and the rabbit-mined, cattle-rubbed posts leaned out and in. A narrow path doubled among the bushes, scores of white tails twinkled before the racing hound, and a hawk rose, whistling shrilly.

'No roads. No nothing!' said Sophie, her short skirt hooked by briers. 'I thought all England was a garden. There's your spire, George, across the valley. How curious!'

They walked toward it through an all-abandoned land. Here they found the ghost of a patch of lucerne that had refused to die; there a harsh fallow surrendered to yard-high thistles; and here a breadth of rampant kelk feigning to be lawful crop. In the ungrazed pastures swathes of dead stuff caught their feet, and the ground beneath glistened with sweat. At the bottom of the valley a little brook had undermined its footbridge, and frothed in the wreckage.   But there stood great woods on the slopes beyond—old, tall, and brilliant, like unfaded tapestries against the walls of a ruined house.

' All this within a hundred miles of London,' he said.   ' Looks as if it had had nervous prostration, too.'   The footpath turned the shoulder of a slope, through a thicket of rank rhododendrons, and crossed what had once been a carriage-drive, which ended in the shadow of two gigantic holm-oaks.

' A house ! ' said Sophie, in a whisper.   ' A colonial house ! '

Behind the blue-green of the twin trees rose a dark-bluish brick Georgian pile, with a shell-shaped fan-light over its pillared door.   The hound had gone off on his own foolish quests. Except for some stir in the branches and the flight of four startled magpies, there was neither life nor sound about the square house, but it looked out of its long windows most friendlily.

' Cha-armed to meet you, I'm sure,' said Sophie, and curtsied to the ground.   ' George, this is history I can understand.   *We* began here.'   She curtsied again.

The June sunshine twinkled on all the lights. It was as though an old lady, wise in three generations' experience, but for the present sitting out, bent to listen to her flushed and eager grandchild.

' I *must* look ! '   Sophie tiptoed to a window, and shaded her eyes with her hand.   ' Oh, this room's half-full of cotton-bales—wool, I suppose !

But I can see a bit of the mantelpiece.   George, do come !   Isn't that some one ? '

She fell back behind her husband.   The front door opened slowly, to show the hound, his nose white with milk, in charge of an ancient of days clad in a blue linen ephod curiously gathered on breast and shoulders.

' Certainly,' said George, half aloud.   ' Father Time himself.   This is where he lives, Sophie.'

' We came—,' said Sophie weakly.   ' Can we see the house?   I'm afraid that's our dog.'

' No, 'tis Rambler,' said the old man.   ' He've been at my swill-pail again.   Staying at Rocketts, be ye?   Come in.   Ah ! you runagate ! '

The hound broke from him, and he tottered after him down the drive.   They entered the hall —just such a high light hall as such a house should own.   A slim-balustered staircase, wide and shallow and once creamy-white, climbed out of it under a long oval window.   On either side delicately-moulded doors gave on to wool-lumbered rooms, whose sea-green mantelpieces were adorned with nymphs, scrolls, and Cupids in low relief.

' What's the firm that makes these things? ' cried Sophie, enraptured.   ' Oh, I forgot ! These must be the originals.   Adams, is it?   I never dreamed of anything like that steel-cut fender. Does he mean us to go everywhere? '

' He's catching the dog,' said George, looking out.   ' We don't count.'

They explored the first or ground floor, delighted as children playing burglars.

'This is like all England,' she said at last.
'Wonderful, but no explanation. You're expected
to know it beforehand. Now let's try upstairs.'

The stairs never creaked beneath their feet.
From the broad landing they entered a long,
green-panelled room lighted by three full-length
windows, which overlooked the forlorn wreck of
a terraced garden, and wooded slopes beyond.

'The drawing-room, of course.' Sophie swam
up and down it. 'That mantelpiece—Orpheus
and Eurydice—is the best of them all. Isn't it
marvellous? Why, the room seems furnished
with nothing in it! How's that, George?'

'It's the proportions. I've noticed it.'

'I saw a Hepplewhite couch once'—Sophie
laid her finger to her flushed cheek and considered. 'With two of them—one on each side
—you wouldn't need anything else. Except—
there must be one perfect mirror over that
mantelpiece.'

'Look at that view. It's a framed Con-
stable,' her husband cried.

'No; it's a Morland—a parody of a Morland.
But about that couch, George. Don't you think
Empire might be better than Hepplewhite? Dull
gold against that pale green? It's a pity they
don't make spinets nowadays.'

'I believe you can get them. Look at that
oak wood behind the pines.'

'"While you sat and played toccatas stately
at the clavichord,"' Sophie hummed, and, head
on one side, nodded to where the perfect mirror
should hang.

B

Then they found bedrooms with dressing-rooms and powdering-closets, and steps leading up and down—boxes of rooms, round, square, and octagonal, with enriched ceilings and chased door-locks.

'Now about servants. Oh!' She had darted up the last stairs to the chequered darkness of the top floor, where loose tiles lay among broken laths, and the walls were scrawled with names, sentiments, and hop-records. 'They've been keeping pigeons here,' she cried.

'And you could drive a buggy through the roof anywhere,' said George.

'That's what *I* say,' the old man cried below them on the stairs. 'Not a dry place for my pigeons at all.'

'But why was it allowed to get like this?' said Sophie.

''Tis with housen as teeth,' he replied. 'Let 'em go too far, and there's nothing *to* be done. Time was they was minded to sell her, but none would buy. She was too far-away-along from any place. Time was they'd ha' lived here theyselves, but they took and died.'

'Here?' Sophie moved beneath the light of a hole in the roof.

'Nah—none dies here excep' falling off ricks and such. In London they died.' He plucked a lock of wool from his blue smock. 'They was no staple—neither the Elphicks nor the Moones. Shart and brittle all of 'em. Dead they be seventeen year, for I've been here caretakin' twenty-five.'

'Who does all the wool belong to downstairs?'
George asked.

'To the estate. I'll show you the back parts
if ye like. You're from America, ain't ye? I've
had a son there once myself.' They followed him
down the main stairway. He paused at the turn
and swept one hand towards the wall. 'Plenty
room here for your coffin to come down. Seven
foot and three men at each end wouldn't brish
the paint. If I die in my bed they'll 'ave to
up-end me like a milk-can. 'Tis all luck, d'ye
see?'

He led them on and on, through a maze of
back-kitchens, dairies, larders, and sculleries, that
melted along covered ways into a farm-house,
visibly older than the main building which, again,
rambled out among barns, byres, pig-pens, stalls
and stables to the dead fields behind.

'Somehow,' said Sophie, sitting exhausted on
an ancient well-curb—'somehow one wouldn't
insult these lovely old things by filling them with
hay.'

George looked at long stone walls upholding
reaches of silvery oak weather-boarding; but-
tresses of mixed flint and bricks; outside stairs,
stone upon arched stone; curves of thatch where
grass sprouted; roundels of house-leeked tiles,
and a huge paved yard populated by two cows
and the repentant Rambler. He had not thought
of himself or of the telegraph office for two and
a half hours.

'But why,' said Sophie, as they went back
through the crater of stricken fields,—'why is one

expected to know everything in England? Why
do they never tell?'

'You mean about the Elphicks and the
Moones?' he answered.

'Yes—and the lawyers and the estate. Who
are they? I wonder whether those painted floors
in the green room were real oak. Don't you
like us exploring things together—better than
Pompeii?'

George turned once more to look at the view.
'Eight hundred acres go with the house—the old
man told me. Five farms altogether. Rocketts is
one of 'em.'

'I like Mrs. Cloke. But what is the old house
called?'

George laughed. 'That's one of the things
you're expected to know. He never told me.'

The Clokes were more communicative. That
evening and thereafter for a week they gave the
Chapins the official history, as one gives it to
lodgers, of Friars Pardon the house and its five
farms. But Sophie asked so many questions, and
George was so humanly interested, that, as confidence in the strangers grew, they launched,
with observed and acquired detail, into the lives
and deaths and doings of the Elphicks and the
Moones and their collaterals, the Haylings and
the Torrells. It was a tale told serially by Cloke
in the barn, or his wife in the dairy, the last
chapters reserved for the kitchen o' nights by the
big fire, when the two had been half the day
exploring about the house, where old Iggulden,
of the blue smock, cackled and chuckled to see

them. The motives that swayed the characters were beyond their comprehension; the fates that shifted them were gods they had never met; the sidelights Mrs. Cloke threw on act and incident were more amazing than anything in the record. Therefore the Chapins listened delightedly, and blessed Mrs. Shonts.

'But why—why—*why*—did So-and-so do so-and-so?' Sophie would demand from her seat by the pothook; and Mrs. Cloke would answer, smoothing her knees, 'For the sake of the place.'

'I give it up,' said George one night in their own room. 'People don't seem to matter in this country compared to the places they live in. The way *she* tells it, Friars Pardon was a sort of Moloch.'

'Poor old thing!' They had been walking round the farms as usual before tea. 'No wonder they loved it. Think of the sacrifices they made for it. Jane Elphick married the younger Torrell to keep it in the family. The octagonal room with the moulded ceiling next to the big bedroom was hers. Now what did *he* tell you while he was feeding the pigs?' said Sophie.

'About the Torrell cousins and the uncle who died in Java. They lived at Burnt House— behind High Pardons, where that brook is all blocked up.'

'No; Burnt House is under High Pardons Wood, *before* you come to Gale Anstey,' Sophie corrected.

'Well, old man Cloke said——'

Sophie threw open the door and called down into the kitchen, where the Clokes were covering the fire: ' Mrs. Cloke, isn't Burnt House under High Pardons?'

' Yes, my dear, of course,' the soft voice answered absently. A cough. ' I beg your pardon, madam. What was it you said?'

' Never mind. I prefer it the other way,' Sophie laughed, and George retold the missing chapter as she sat on the bed.

' Here to-day an' gone to-morrow,' said Cloke warningly. ' They've paid their first month, but we've only that Mrs. Shonts' letter for guarantee.'

' None she sent never cheated us yet. It slipped out before I thought. She's a most humane young lady. They'll be going away in a little. An' *you*'ve talked a lot too, Alfred.'

' Yes, but the Elphicks are all dead. No one can bring my loose talking home to me. But why do they stay on and stay on so?'

In due time George and Sophie asked each other that question, and put it aside. They argued that the climate—a pearly blend, unlike the hot and cold ferocities of their native land— suited them, as the thick stillness of the nights certainly suited George. He was saved even the sight of a metalled road, which, as presumably leading to business, wakes desire in a man; and the telegraph office at the village of Friars Pardon, where they sold picture post-cards and peg-tops, was two walking miles across the fields and woods. For all that touched his past among his fellows, or their remembrance of him, he might have been in another planet; and Sophie, whose life had been very largely spent among husbandless wives of lofty ideals, had no wish to leave this present of God. The unhurried meals, the foreknowledge of deliciously empty hours to follow, the breadths of soft sky under which they walked together and reckoned time only by their hunger or thirst; the good grass beneath their feet that cheated the miles; their discoveries, always together, amid the farms—Griffons, Rocketts, Burnt House, Gale Anstey, and the Home Farm, where Iggulden of the blue smock-frock would waylay them, and they would ransack the old house once more; the long wet afternoons when they tucked up their feet on the bedroom's deep window-sill over against the apple-trees, and talked together as never till then had they found time to talk—these things contented her soul, and her body throve.

'Have you realised,' she asked one morning, 'that we've been here absolutely alone for the last thirty-four days?'

'Have you counted them?' he asked.

'Did you like them?' she replied.

'I must have. I didn't think about them. Yes, I have. Six months ago I should have fretted myself sick. Remember at Cairo? I've only had two or three bad times. Am I getting better, or is it senile decay?'

'Climate, all climate.' Sophie swung her new-bought English boots, as she sat on the stile overlooking Friars Pardon, behind the Clokes' barn.

'One must take hold of things, though,' he said, ' if it's only to keep one's hand in.' His eyes did not flicker now as they swept the empty fields. ' Mustn't one? '

'Lay out a Morristown links over Gale Anstey? I dare say you could hire it.'

' No, I'm not as English as that—nor as Morristown. Cloke says all the farms here could be made to pay.'

' Well, I'm Anastasia in the *Treasure of Franchard*. I'm content to be alive and purr. There's no hurry.'

' No.' He smiled. ' All the same, I'm going to see after my mail.'

' You promised you wouldn't have any.'

' There's some business coming through that's amusing me. Honest. It doesn't get on my nerves at all.'

' Want a secretary? '

' No, thanks, old thing! Isn't that quite English? '

'Too English! Go away.' But none the less in broad daylight she returned the kiss. ' I'm off to Pardons. I haven't been to the house for nearly a week.'

' How've you decided to furnish Jane Elphick's bedroom? ' he laughed, for it had come to be a permanent Castle in Spain between them.

' Black Chinese furniture and yellow silk brocade,' she answered, and ran downhill. She scattered a few cows at a gap with a flourish of a ground-ash that Iggulden had cut for her a week ago, and singing as she passed under the holm-oaks, sought the farm-house at the back of Friars Pardon. The old man was not to be found, and she knocked at his half-opened door, for she needed him to fill her idle forenoon. A blue-eyed sheep-dog, a new friend, and Rambler's old enemy, crawled out and besought her to enter.

Iggulden sat in his chair by the fire, a thistle-spud between his knees, his head drooped. Though she had never seen death before, her heart, that missed a beat, told her that he was dead. She did not speak or cry, but stood outside the door, and the dog licked her hand. When he threw up his nose, she heard herself saying : ' Don't howl ! Please don't begin to howl, Scottie, or I shall run away ! '

She held her ground while the shadows in the rickyard moved toward noon ; sat after a while on the steps by the door, her arms round the dog's neck, waiting till some one should come. She watched the smokeless chimneys of Friars Pardon slash its roofs with shadow, and the smoke of Iggulden's last lighted fire gradually thin and cease. Against her will she fell to wondering how many Moones, Elphicks, and Torrells had been swung round the turn of the broad hall stairs. Then she remembered the old man's talk of being ' up-ended like a milk-can,' and buried her face on Scottie's neck. At last a horse's feet clinked upon flags, rustled in the old grey straw of the rickyard, and she found herself facing the Vicar— a figure she had seen at church declaiming im-possibilities (Sophie was a Unitarian) in an unnatural voice.

' He's dead,' she said, without preface.

'Old Iggulden? I was coming for a talk with him.' The Vicar passed in uncovered. ' Ah ! ' she heard him say. ' Heart-failure ! How long have you been here? '

' Since a quarter to eleven.' She looked at her watch earnestly and saw that her hand did not shake.

' I'll sit with him now till the doctor comes. D'you think you could tell him, and—yes, Mrs. Betts in the cottage with the wistaria next the blacksmith's? I'm afraid this has been rather a shock to you.'

Sophie nodded, and fled toward the village. Her body failed her for a moment ; she dropped beneath a hedge, and looked back at the great house. In some fashion its silence and stolidity steadied her for her errand.

Mrs. Betts, small, black-eyed and dark, was almost as unconcerned as Friars Pardon.

' Yiss, yiss, of course. Dear me ! Well, Iggulden he had had his day in my father's time. Muriel, get me my little blue bag, please. Yiss, ma'am. They come down like ellum-branches in still weather. No warnin' *at* all. Muriel, my bicycle's be'ind the fowl-house. I'll tell Dr. Dallas, ma'am.'

She trundled off on her wheel like a brown bee, while Sophie—heaven above and earth beneath changed—walked stiffly home, to fall over George at his letters, in a muddle of laughter and tears.

' It's all quite natural for *them*,' she gasped.

' " They come down like ellum-branches in still weather. Yiss, ma'am." No, there wasn't anything in the least horrible, only—only—Oh, George, that poor shiny stick of his between his poor, thin knees ! I couldn't have borne it if Scottie had howled. I didn't know the Vicar was so—so sensitive. He said he was afraid it was ra-rather a shock. Mrs. Betts told me to go home, and I wanted to collapse on her floor. But I didn't disgrace myself. I—I couldn't have left him— could I ? '

' You're sure you've took no 'arm ? ' cried Mrs. Cloke, who had heard the news by farm-tele-graphy, which is older but swifter than Marconi's.

' No. I'm perfectly well,' Sophie protested.

' You lay down till tea-time.' Mrs. Cloke patted her shoulder. ' *They*'ll be very pleased, though she 'as 'ad no proper understandin' for twenty years.'

' They ' came before twilight — a black-bearded man in moleskins, and a little palsied old woman, who chirruped like a wren.

' I'm his son,' said the man to Sophie, among the lavender bushes. ' We 'ad a difference— twenty year back—and didn't speak since. But I'm his son all the same, and we thank you for the watching.'

' I'm only glad I happened to be there,' she answered, and from the bottom of her heart she meant it.

' We heard he spoke a lot o' you—one time an' another since you came. We thank you kindly,' the man added.

' Are you the son that was in America?' she asked.

' Yes, ma'am. On my uncle's farm, in Connecticut. He was what they call road-master there.'

' Whereabouts in Connecticut?' asked George over her shoulder.

' Veering Holler was the name. I was there six year with my uncle.'

' How small the world is!' Sophie cried. ' Why, all my mother's people come from Veering Hollow. There must be some there still—the Lashmars. Did you ever hear of them?'

' I remember hearing that name, seems to me,' he answered, but his face was blank as the back of a spade.

A little before dusk a woman in grey, striding like a foot-soldier, and bearing on her arm a long pole, crashed through the orchard calling for food. George, upon whom the unannounced English worked mysteriously, fled to the parlour; but Mrs. Cloke came forward beaming. Sophie could not escape.

' We've only just heard of it,' said the stranger, turning on her. ' I've been out with the otter-hounds all day. It was a splendidly sportin' thing——'

' Did you—er—kill?' said Sophie. She knew from books she could not go far wrong here.

' Yes, a dry bitch—seventeen pounds,' was the answer. ' A splendidly sportin' thing of you to do. Poor old Iggulden——'

' Oh—that ! ' said Sophie, enlightened.

' If there had been any people at Pardons it would never have happened. He'd have been looked after. But what can you expect from a parcel of London solicitors? '

Mrs. Cloke murmured something.

' No. I'm soaked from the knees down. If I hang about I shall get chilled. A cup of tea, Mrs. Cloke, and I can eat one of your sandwiches as I go.' She wiped her weather-worn face with a green-and-yellow silk handkerchief.

' Yes, my lady ! ' Mrs. Cloke ran and returned swiftly.

' Our land marches with Pardons for a mile on the south,' she explained, waving the full cup, ' but one has quite enough to do with one's own people without poachin'. Still, if I'd known, I'd have sent Dora, of course. Have you seen her this afternoon, Mrs. Cloke? No? I wonder whether that girl *did* sprain her ankle. Thank you.' It was a formidable hunk of bread and bacon that Mrs. Cloke presented. ' As I was sayin', Pardons is a scandal ! Lettin' people die like dogs. There ought to be people there who do their duty. You've done yours, though there wasn't the faintest call upon you. Good night. Tell Dora, if she comes, I've gone on.'

She strode away, munching her crust, and Sophie reeled breathless into the parlour, to shake the shaking George.

' Why did you keep catching my eye behind the blind? Why didn't you come out and do your duty? '

'Because I should have burst. Did you see the mud on its cheek?' he said.

'Once. I daren't look again. Who is she?'

'God. A local deity then. Anyway, she's another of the things you're expected to know by instinct.'

Mrs. Cloke, shocked at their levity, told them that it was Lady Conant, wife of Sir Walter Conant, Baronet, a large landholder in the neighbourhood, and if not God, at least His visible Providence.

George made her talk of that family for an hour.

'Laughter,' said Sophie afterward in their own room, 'is the mark of the savage. Why couldn't you control your emotions? It's all real to *her*.'

'It's all real to *me*. That's my trouble,' he answered in an altered tone. 'Anyway, it's real enough to mark time with. Don't you think so?'

'What d'you mean?' she asked quickly, though she knew his voice.

'That I'm better. I'm well enough to kick.'

'What at?'

'This!' He waved his hand round the one room. 'I must have something to play with till I'm fit for work again.'

'Ah!' She sat on the bed and leaned forward, her hands clasped. 'I wonder if it's good for you.'

'We've been better here than anywhere,' he went on slowly. 'One could always sell it again.'

She nodded gravely, but her eyes sparkled.

'The only thing that worries me is what

happened this morning. I want to know how you
feel about it. If it's on your nerves in the least
we can have the old farm at the back of the house
pulled down, or perhaps it has spoiled the notion
for you?'

'Pull it down?' she cried. 'You've no business faculty. Why, that's where we could live
while we're putting the big house in order. It's
almost under the same roof. No! What happened
this morning seemed to be more of a—of a leading
than anything else. There *ought* to be people
at Pardons. Lady Conant's quite right.'

'I was thinking more of the woods and the
roads. I could double the value of the place in
six months.'

'What do they want for it?' She shook her
head, and her loosened hair fell glowingly about
her cheeks.

'Seventy-five thousand dollars. They'll take
sixty-eight.'

'Less than half what we paid for our old
yacht when we married. And we didn't have a
good time in her. You were——'

'Well, I discovered I was too much of an
American to be content to be a rich man's son.
You aren't blaming me for that?'

'Oh no. Only it was a very businesslike honeymoon. How far are you along with the deal,
George?'

'I can mail the deposit on the purchase money
to-morrow morning, and we can have the thing
completed in a fortnight or three weeks—if you
say so.'

'Friars Pardon—Friars Pardon!' Sophie chanted rapturously, her dark-grey eyes big with delight. 'All the farms? Gale Anstey, Burnt House, Rocketts, the Home Farm, and Griffons? Sure you've got 'em all?'

'Sure.' He smiled.

'And the woods? High Pardons Wood, Lower Pardons, Suttons, Dutton's Shaw, Reuben's Ghyll, Maxey's Ghyll, and both the Oak Hangers? Sure you've got 'em all?'

'Every last stick. Why, you know them as well as I do.' He laughed. 'They say there's five thousand—a thousand pounds' worth of lumber—timber they call it—in the Hangers alone.'

'Mrs. Cloke's oven must be mended first thing, *and* the kitchen roof. I think I'll have all this whitewashed,' Sophie broke in, pointing to the ceiling. 'The whole place is a scandal. Lady Conant is quite right. George, when did you begin to fall in love with the house? In the green room—that first day? I did.'

'I'm not in love with it. One must do something to mark time till one's fit for work.'

'Or when we stood under the oaks, and the door opened? Oh! Ought I to go to poor Iggulden's funeral?' She sighed with utter happiness.

'Wouldn't they call it a liberty—*now*?' said he.

'But I liked him.'

'But you didn't own him at the date of his death.'

'That wouldn't keep me away. Only, they

made such a fuss about the watching '—she caught her breath—' it might be ostentatious from that point of view, too.   Oh, George,'—she reached for his hand—' we're two little orphans moving in worlds not realised, and we shall make some bad breaks.   But we're going to have the time of our lives.'

' We'll run up to London to-morrow and see if we can hurry those English law— solicitors.   I want to get to work.'

They went.   They suffered many things ere they returned across the fields in a fly one Saturday night, nursing a two by two-and-a-half box of deeds and maps—lawful owners of Friars Pardon and the five decayed farms therewith.

' I do most sincerely 'ope and trust you'll be 'appy, madam,' Mrs. Cloke gasped, when she was told the news by the kitchen fire.

' Goodness !   It isn't a marriage ! ' Sophie exclaimed, a little awed ; for to them the joke, which to an American means work, was only just beginning.

' If it's took in a proper spirit '—Mrs. Cloke's eye turned toward her oven.

' Send and have that mended to-morrow,' Sophie whispered.

' We couldn't 'elp noticing,' said Cloke slowly, ' from the times you walked there, that you an' your lady was drawn to it, but—but I don't know as we ever precisely thought——' His wife's glance checked him.

' That we were that sort of people,' said George.   ' We aren't sure of it ourselves yet.'

c

' Perhaps,' said Cloke, rubbing his knees, just for the sake of saying something, ' perhaps you'll park it?'

' What's that?' said George.

' Turn it all into a fine park like Violet Hill '— he jerked a thumb to westward—'that Mr. Sangres bought. It was four farms, and Mr. Sangres made a fine park of them, with a herd of faller deer.'

' Then it wouldn't be Friars Pardon,' said Sophie. ' Would it?'

' I don't know as I've ever heard Pardons was ever anything but wheat an' wool. Only some gentlemen say that parks are less trouble than tenants.' He laughed nervously. ' But the gentry, o' course, they keep on pretty much as they was used to.'

' I see,' said Sophie. ' How did Mr. Sangres make his money?'

' I never rightly heard. It was pepper an' spices, or it may ha' been gloves. No. Gloves was Sir Reginald Liss at Marley End. Spices was Mr. Sangres. He's a Brazilian gentleman— very sunburnt, like.'

' Be sure o' one thing. You won't 'ave any trouble,' said Mrs. Cloke, just before they went to bed.

Now the news of the purchase was told to Mr. and Mrs. Cloke alone at 8 P.M. of a Saturday. None left the farm till they set out for church next morning. Yet when they reached the church and were about to slip aside into their usual seats, a little beyond the font, where they could see the red-furred tails of the bell-ropes waggle and twist at ringing-time, they were swept forward irresistibly, a Cloke on either flank (and yet they had not walked with the Clokes), upon the ever-retiring bosom of a black-gowned verger, who ushered them into a room of a pew at the head of the left aisle, under the pulpit.

' This,' he sighed reproachfully, ' is the Pardons' Pew,' and shut them in.

They could see little more than the choir-boys in the chancel, but to the roots of the hair of their necks they felt the congregation behind mercilessly devouring them by look.

' *When the wicked man turneth away.*'   The strong alien voice of the priest vibrated under the hammer-beam roof, and a loneliness unfelt before swamped their hearts, as they searched for places in the unfamiliar Church of England service. The Lord's Prayer—' Our Father, *which* art '— set the seal on that desolation.   Sophie found herself thinking how in other lands their purchase would long ere this have been discussed from every point of view in a dozen prints, forgetting that George for months had not been allowed to glance at those black and bellowing head-lines. Here was nothing but silence—not even hostility ! The game was up to them.   The other players hid their cards and waited.   Suspense, she felt, was in the air, and when her sight cleared, she saw indeed a mural tablet of a footless bird brooding upon the carven motto, ' Wayte awhyle—wayte awhyle.'

At the Litany George had trouble with an

unstable hassock, and drew the slip of carpet under the pew-seat. Sophie pushed her end back also, and shut her eyes against a burning that felt like tears. When she opened them she was looking at her mother's maiden name, fairly carved on a blue flagstone on the pew floor :—

Ellen Lashmar . ob. 1796 . aetat. 27.

She nudged George and pointed. Sheltered, as they kneeled, they looked for more knowledge, but the rest of the slab was blank.

' Ever hear of her? ' he whispered.

' Never knew any of us came from here.'

' Coincidence? '

' Perhaps. But it makes me feel better,' and she smiled and winked away a tear on her lashes, and took his hand while they prayed for ' all women labouring of child '—not ' in the perils of childbirth '; and the sparrows who had found their way through the guards behind the stained-glass windows chirped above the faded gilt-and-alabaster family tree of the Conants.

The baronet's pew was on the right of the aisle. After service its inhabitants moved forth without haste, but so as to effectively block a dusky person with a large family who champed in their rear.

' Spices, I think,' said Sophie, deeply delighted as the Sangres closed up after the Conants. ' Let 'em get away, George.'

But when they came out many folk whose eyes were one still lingered by the lych-gate.

' I want to see if any more Lashmars are

buried here,' said Sophie.

' Not now. This seems to be show day. Come home quickly,' he replied.

A group of families, the Clokes a little apart, opened to let them through. The men saluted with jerky nods, the women with remnants of a curtsey. Only Iggulden's son, his mother on his arm, lifted his hat as Sophie passed.

' Your people?' said the clear voice of Lady Conant in her ear.

' I suppose so,' said Sophie, blushing, for they were within two yards of her; but it was not a question.

' Then that child looks as if it were coming down with mumps. You ought to tell the mother she shouldn't have brought it to church.'

' I can't leave 'er be'ind, my lady,' the woman said. ' She'd set the 'ouse afire in a minute, she's that forward with the matches. Ain't you, Maudie dear?'

' Has Dr. Dallas seen her?'

' Not yet, my lady.'

' He must. You can't get away, of course. M—m! My idiotic maid is coming in for her teeth to-morrow at twelve. She shall pick her up—at Gale Anstey, isn't it?—at eleven.'

' Yes. Thank you very much, my lady.'

' I oughtn't to have done it,' said Lady Conant apologetically, ' but there has been no one at Pardons for so long that you'll forgive my poachin'. Now, can't you lunch with us? The Vicar usually comes too. I don't use the horses on a Sunday,'—she glanced at the Brazilian's silver-plated chariot. ' It's only a mile across the fields.'

' You—you're very kind,' said Sophie, hating herself because her lip trembled.

' My dear '—the compelling tone dropped to a soothing gurgle—' d'you suppose I don't know how it feels to come to a strange county—country, I should say—away from one's own people? When I first left the Shires—I'm Shropshire, you know—I cried for a day and a night. But fretting doesn't make loneliness any better. Oh, here's Dora. She *did* sprain her leg that day.'

' I'm as lame as a tree still,' said the tall maiden frankly. ' You ought to go out with the otter-hounds, Mrs. Chapin. I believe they're drawing your water next week.'

Sir Walter had already led off George, and the Vicar came up on the other side of Sophie. There was no escaping the swift procession or the leisurely lunch, where talk came and went in low-voiced eddies that had the village for their centre. Sophie heard the Vicar and Sir Walter address her husband lightly as Chapin! (She also remembered many women known in a previous life who habitually addressed their husbands as Mr. Such-an-one.) After lunch Lady Conant talked to her explicitly of maternity as that is achieved in cottages and farm-houses remote from aid, and of the duty thereto of the mistress of Pardons.

A gate in a beech hedge, reached across triple lawns, let them out before tea-time into the unkempt south side of their land.

' I want your hand, please,' said Sophie as soon as they were safe among the beech-boles and the

lawless hollies. 'D'you remember the old maid
in *Providence and the Guitar* who heard the Com-
missary swear, and hardly reckoned herself a
maiden lady afterwards? Because I'm a relative
of hers. Lady Conant is——'

'Did you find out anything about the Lashmars?' he interrupted.

'I didn't ask. I'm going to write to Aunt
Sydney about it first. Oh, Lady Conant said
something at lunch about their having bought
some land from some Lashmars a few years ago.
I found it was at the beginning of last century.'

'What did you say?'

'I said, "Really, how interesting!" Like
that. I'm not going to push myself forward. I've
been hearing about Mr. Sangres' efforts in that
direction. And you? I couldn't see you behind
the flowers. Was it very deep water, dear?'

George mopped a brow already browned by
outdoor exposure.

'Oh no—dead easy,' he answered. 'I've
bought Friars Pardon to prevent Sir Walter's
birds straying.'

A cock pheasant scuttered through the dry
leaves and exploded almost under their feet.
Sophie jumped.

'That's one of 'em,' said George calmly.

'Well, your nerves are better, at any rate,' said
she. 'Did you tell 'em you'd bought the thing
to play with?'

'No. That was where my nerve broke down.
I only made one bad break—I think. I said I
couldn't see why hiring land to men to farm wasn't

as much a business proposition as anything else.'

'And what did they say?'

'They smiled. I shall know what that smile means some day. They don't waste their smiles. D'you see that track by Gale Anstey?'

They looked down from the edge of the hanger over a cup-like hollow. People by twos and threes in their Sunday best filed slowly along the paths that connected farm to farm.

'I've never seen so many on our land before,' said Sophie. 'Why is it?'

'To show us we mustn't shut up their rights of way.'

'Those cow-tracks we've been using cross-lots?' said Sophie forcibly.

'Yes. Any one of 'em would cost us two thousand pounds each in legal expenses to close.'

'But we don't want to,' she said.

'The whole community would fight if we did.'

'But it's our land. We can do what we like.'

'It's *not* our land. We've only paid for it. We belong to it, and it belongs to the people— our people, they call 'em. *I*'ve been to lunch with the English too.'

They passed slowly from one bracken-dotted field to the next—flushed with pride of owner-ship, plotting alterations and restorations at each turn ; halting in their tracks to argue, spreading apart to embrace two views at once, or closing in to consider one. Couples moved out of their way, but smiling covertly.

'We shall make some bad breaks,' he said at last.

' Together, though. You won't let any one else in, will you? '

' Except the contractors. This syndicate handles this proposition by its little lone.'

' But you might feel the want of some one,' she insisted.

' I shall—but it will be you. It's business, Sophie, but it's going to be good fun.'

' Please God,' she answered, flushing, and cried to herself as they went back to tea. ' It's worth it. Oh, it's worth it.'

The repairing and moving into Friars Pardon was business of the most varied and searching, but all done English-fashion, without friction. Time and money alone were asked. The rest lay in the hands of beneficent advisers from London, or spirits, male and female, called up by Mr. and Mrs. Cloke from the wastes of the farms. In the centre stood George and Sophie, a little aghast, their interests reaching out on every side.

' I ain't sayin' anything against Londoners,' said Cloke, self-appointed Clerk of the outer works, consulting engineer, head of the immigration bureau, and superintendent of Woods and Forests ; ' but your own people won't go about to make more than a fair profit out of you.'

' How is one to know? ' said George.

' Five years from now, or so on, maybe, you'll be lookin' over your first year's accounts, and, knowin' what you'll know then, you'll say : " Well, Billy Beartup "—or Old Cloke as it might be— " did me proper when I was new." No man likes to have that sort of thing laid up against him.'

'I think I see,' said George. 'But five years is a long time to look ahead.'

'I doubt if that oak Billy Beartup throwed in Reuben's Ghyll will be fit for her drawin'-room floor in less than seven,' Cloke drawled.

'Yes, that's *my* work,' said Sophie. (Billy Beartup of Griffons, a woodman by training and birth, a tenant farmer by misfortune of marriage, had laid his broad axe at her feet a month before.) 'Sorry if I've committed you to another eternity.'

'And we shan't even know where we've gone wrong with *your* new carriage-drive before that time either,' said Cloke, ever anxious to keep the balance true—with an ounce or two in Sophie's favour. The past four months had taught George better than to reply. The carriage-road winding up the hill was his present keen interest. They set off to look at it, and the imported American scraper, which had blighted the none too sunny soul of 'Skim' Winsh, the carter. But young Iggulden was in charge now, and under his guidance Buller and Roberts, the great horses, moved mountains.

'You lif' her like that, an' you tip her like that,' he explained to the gang. 'My uncle he was road-master in Connecticut.'

'Are they roads yonder?' said Skim, sitting under the laurels.

'No better than accommodation-roads. Dirt, they call 'em. They'd suit you, Skim.'

'Why?' said the incautious Skim.

''Cause you'd take no hurt when you fall out

of your cart drunk on a Saturday,' was the answer.

' I didn't last time neither,' Skim roared.

After the loud laugh, old Whybarne of Gale Anstey piped feebly, ' Well, dirt or no dirt, there's no denyin' Chapin knows a good job when he sees it. 'E don't build one day and dee-stroy the next, like that nigger Sangres.'

' *She*'s the one that knows her own mind,' said Pinky, brother to Skim Winsh, and a Napoleon among carters who had helped to bring the grand piano across the fields in the autumn rains.

' She had ought to,' said Iggulden. ' Whoa, Buller ! She's a Lashmar. They never was double-thinking.'

' Oh, you found that ? Has the answer come from your uncle ? ' said Skim, doubtful whether so remote a land as America had posts.

The others looked at him scornfully. Skim was always a day behind the fair.

Iggulden rested from his labours. ' She's a Lashmar right enough. I started up to write to my uncle at once—the month after she said her folks came from Veerin' Holler.'

' Where there ain't any roads ? ' Skim interrupted, but none laughed.

' My uncle he married an American woman for his second, and she took it up like a—like the coroner. She's a Lashmar out of the old Lashmar place, 'fore they sold to Conants. She ain't no Toot Hill Lashmar, nor any o' the Crayford lot. Her folk come out of the ground here, neither Chalk nor Forest, but Wildishers. They sailed

over to America—I've got it all writ down by
my uncle's woman—in eighteen hundred an'
nothing. My uncle says they're all slow begetters,
like.'

'Would they be gentry yonder now?' Skim
asked.

'Nah—there's no gentry in America, no
matter how long you're there. It's against their
law. There's only rich and poor allowed. They've
been lawyers and such-like over yonder for a
hundred years—but she's a Lashmar for all that.'

'Lord! What's a hundred years?' said Whybarne, who had seen seventy-eight of them.

'An' they write too, from yonder—my uncle's
woman writes—that you can still tell 'em by head-
mark.   Their hair's foxy-red still—an' they
throw out when they walk. *He*'s in-toed—treads
like a gipsy; but you watch, an' you'll see 'er
throw out—like a colt.'

'Your trace wants taking up.' Pinky's large
ears had caught the sound of voices, and as the
two broke through the laurels the men were hard
at work, their eyes on Sophie's feet.

She had been less fortunate in her inquiries
than Iggulden, for her Aunt Sydney of Meriden
(a badged and certificated Daughter of the Revolution to boot) answered her inquiries with a
two-paged discourse on patriotism, the leaflets of
a Village Improvement Society, of which she was
president, and a demand for an overdue sub-
scription to a Factory Girls' Reading Circle.
Sophie burned it all in the Orpheus and Eurydice
grate, and kept her own counsel.

'What *I* want to know,' said George, when spring was coming, and the gardens needed thought, ' is who will ever pay me for my labour? I've put in at least half a million dollars' worth already.'

' Sure you're not taking too much out of yourself?' his wife asked.

' Oh no; I haven't been conscious of myself all winter.' He looked at his brown English gaiters and smiled. ' It's all behind me now. I believe I could sit down and think of all that—those months before we sailed.'

' Don't—ah, don't!' she cried.

' But I must go back one day. You don't want to keep me out of business always—or do you?' He ended with a nervous laugh.

Sophie sighed as she drew her own ground-ash (of old Iggulden's cutting) from the hall rack.

' Aren't you overdoing it too? You look a little tired,' he said.

' You make me tired. I'm going to Rocketts to see Mrs. Cloke about Mary.' (This was the sister of the telegraphist, promoted to be sewing-maid at Pardons.)   ' Coming?'

' I'm due at Burnt House to see about the new well. By the way, there's a sore throat at Gale Anstey——'

' That's *my* province. Don't interfere. The Whybarne children always have sore throats. They do it for jujubes.'

' Keep away from Gale Anstey till I make sure, honey.   Cloke ought to have told me.'

' These people don't tell. Haven't you learnt

that yet? But I'll obey, me lord. See you later!'

She set off afoot, for within the three main roads that bounded the blunt triangle of the estate (even by night one could scarcely hear the carts on them), wheels were not used except for farm work. The footpaths served all other purposes. And though at first they had planned improvements, they had soon fallen in with the customs of their hidden kingdom, and moved about the soft-footed ways by woodland, hedge-row, and shaw as freely as the rabbits. Indeed, for the most part Sophie walked bareheaded beneath her helmet of chestnut hair; but she had been plagued of late by vague toothaches, which she explained to Mrs. Cloke, who asked some questions. How it came about Sophie never knew, but after a while behold Mrs. Cloke's arm was about her waist, and her head was on that deep bosom behind the shut kitchen door.

'My dear! my dear!' the elder woman almost sobbed. 'An' d'you mean to tell me you never suspicioned? Why—why—where *was* you ever taught anything at all? Of *course* it is. It's what we've been only waitin' for, all of us. Time and again I've said to Lady——' She checked herself. 'An' now we shall be as we should be.'

'But—but—but——' Sophie whimpered.

'An' to see you buildin' your nest so busy—pianos and books—an' never thinkin' of a nursery!'

'No more I did.' Sophie sat bolt upright, and began to laugh.

'Time enough yet.' The fingers tapped

thoughtfully on the broad knee. 'But—they must be strange-minded folk over yonder with you! Have you thought to send for your mother? She dead? My dear, my dear! Never mind! She'll be happy where she knows. 'Tis God's work. An' we was only waitin' for it, for you've never failed in your duty yet. It ain't your way. *What* did you say about my Mary's doings?' Mrs. Cloke's face hardened as she pressed her chin on Sophie's forehead. 'If any of your girls thinks to be'ave arbitrary now, I'll—— But they won't, my dear. I'll see they do their duty too. Be sure you'll 'ave no trouble.'

When Sophie walked back across the fields, heaven and earth changed about her as on the days of old Iggulden's death. For an instant she thought of the wide turn of the staircase, and the new ivory-white paint that no coffin-corner could scar, but presently the shadow passed in a pure wonder and bewilderment that made her reel. She leaned against one of their new gates and looked over their lands for some other stay.

'Well,' she said resignedly, half aloud, 'we must try to make him feel that he isn't a third in our party,' and turned the corner that looked over Friars Pardon, giddy, sick, and faint.

Of a sudden the house they had bought for a whim stood up as she had never seen it before, low-fronted, broad-winged, ample, prepared by course of generations for all such things. As it had steadied her when it lay desolate, so now that it had meaning from their few months of life within, it soothed and promised good. She went alone and quickly into the hall, and kissed either door-post, whispering: ' Be good to me. *You* know! You've never failed in your duty yet.'

When the matter was explained to George, he would have sailed at once to their own land, but this Sophie forbade.

' I don't want science,' she said. ' I just want to be loved, and there isn't time for that at home. Besides,' she added, looking out of the window, ' it would be desertion.'

George was forced to soothe himself with linking Friars Pardon to the telegraph system of Great Britain by telephone—three-quarters of a mile of poles, put in by Whybarne and a few friends. One of these was a foreigner from the next parish. Said he when the line was being run: ' There's an old ellum right in our road. Shall us throw her? '

' Toot Hill parish folk, neither grace nor good luck, God help 'em.' Old Whybarne shouted the local proverb from three poles down the line. ' *We* ain't goin' to lay any axe-iron to coffin-wood here—not till we know where we are yet awhile. Swing round 'er, swing round! '

To this day, then, that sudden kink in the straight line across the upper pasture remains a mystery to Sophie and George. Nor can they tell why Skim Winsh, who came to his cottage under Dutton Shaw most musically drunk at 10.45 P.M. of every Saturday night, as his father had done before him, sang no more at the bottom of the garden steps, where Sophie always feared he

would break his neck. The path was undoubtedly
an ancient right of way, and at 10.45 P.M. on
Saturdays Skim remembered it was his duty to
posterity to keep it open—till Mrs. Cloke spoke
to him—once. She spoke likewise to her daughter
Mary, sewing-maid at Pardons, and to Mary's
best new friend, the five-foot-seven imported
London house-maid, who taught Mary to trim
hats, and found the country dullish.

But there was no noise,—at no time was there
any noise,—and when Sophie walked abroad she
met no one in her path unless she had signified
a wish that way. Then they appeared to protest
that all was well with them and their children,
their chickens, their roofs, their water-supply, and
their sons in the Police or the railway service.

' But don't you find it dull, dear? ' said George,
loyally doing his best not to worry as the months
went by.

' I've been so busy putting my house in order
I haven't had time to think,' said she. ' Do
you? '

' No—no. If I could only be sure of *you*.'

She turned on the green drawing-room's couch
(it was Empire, not Hepplewhite after all), and
laid aside a list of linen and blankets.

' It has changed everything, hasn't it? ' she
whispered.

' Oh Lord, yes. But I still think if we went
back to Baltimore——'

' And missed our first real summer together.
No, thank you, me lord.'

' But we're absolutely alone.'

D

' Isn't that what I'm doing my best to remedy? Don't you worry. I like it—like it to the marrow of my little bones. You don't realise what her house means to a woman. We thought we were living in it last year, but we hadn't begun to. Don't you rejoice in your study, George?'

' I prefer being here with you.' He sat down on the floor by the couch and took her hand.

' Seven,' she said as the French clock struck. ' Year before last you'd just be coming back from business.'

He winced at the recollection, then laughed. ' Business! I've been at work ten solid hours to-day.'

' Where did you lunch?   With the Conants?'

' No ; at Dutton Shaw, sitting on a log, with my feet in a swamp. But we've found out where the old spring is, and we're going to pipe it down to Gale Anstey next year.'

' I'll come and see to-morrow. Oh, please open the door, dear. I want to look down the passage. Isn't that corner by the stair-head lovely where the sun strikes in?' She looked through half-closed eyes at the vista of ivory-white and pale green all steeped in liquid gold.

' There's a step out of Jane Elphick's bed-room,' she went on—' and *his* first step in the world ought to be up. I shouldn't wonder if those people hadn't put it there on purpose. George, will it make any odds to you if he's a girl?'

He answered, as he had many times before, that his interest was his wife, not the child.

'Then you're the only person who thinks so.'
She laughed. 'Don't be silly, dear. It's expected.
I know. It's my duty. I shan't be able to look
our people in the face if I fail.'

'What concern is it of theirs, confound 'em!'

'You'll see. Luckily the tradition of the house
is boys, Mrs. Cloke says, so I'm provided for.
Shall you ever begin to understand these people?
I shan't.'

'And we bought it for fun—for fun?' he
groaned. 'And here we are held up for goodness
knows how long!'

'Why? Were you thinking of selling it?'
He did not answer. 'Do you remember the
second Mrs. Chapin?' she demanded.

This was a bold, brazen little black-browed
woman—a widow for choice—who on Sophie's
death was guilefully to marry George for his
wealth and ruin him in a year. George being
busy, Sophie had invented her some two years
after her marriage, and conceived she was alone
among wives in so doing.

'You aren't going to bring *her* up again?' he
asked anxiously.

'I only want to say that I should hate any one
who bought Pardons ten times worse than I used
to hate the second Mrs. Chapin. Think what
we've put into it of our two selves.'

'At least a couple of million dollars. I know
I could have made——' He broke off.

'The beasts!' she went on. 'They'd be sure
to build a red-brick lodge at the gates, and cut
the lawn up for bedding out. You must leave

instructions in your will that *he*'s never to do that,
George, won't you?'

He laughed and took her hand again but said
nothing till it was time to dress. Then he
muttered: 'What the devil use is a man's
country to him when he can't do business in
it?'

Friars Pardon stood faithful to its tradition.
At the appointed time was born, not that third in
their party to whom Sophie meant to be so kind,
but a godling; in beauty, it was manifest, excelling
Eros, as in wisdom Confucius; an enhancer of
delights, a renewer of companionships and an
interpreter of Destiny. This last George did not
realise till he met Lady Conant striding through
Dutton Shaw a few days after the event.

'My dear fellow,' she cried, and slapped him
heartily on the back, 'I can't tell you how glad we
all are.—Oh, *she*'ll be all right. (There's never
been any trouble over the birth of an heir at
Pardons.) Now where the dooce is it?' She
felt largely in her leather-bound skirt and drew
out a small silver mug. 'I sent a note to your
wife about it, but my silly ass of a groom forgot
to take this. You can save me a tramp. Give her
my love.' She marched off amid her guard of
grave Airedales.

The mug was worn and dented: above the
twined initials, G. L., was the crest of a footless
bird and the motto: 'Wayte awhyle—wayte
awhyle.'

'That's the other end of the riddle,' Sophie

whispered, when he saw her that evening. ' Read her note. The English write beautiful notes.'

The warmest of welcomes to your little man. I hope he will appreciate his native land now he has come to it. Though you have said nothing we cannot, of course, look on him as a little stranger, and so I am sending him the old Lashmar christening mug. It has been with us since Gregory Lashmar, your great-grandmother's brother—

George stared at his wife.
' Go on,' she twinkled from the pillows.

—mother's brother, sold his place to Walter's family. We seem to have acquired some of your household gods at that time, but nothing survives except the mug and the old cradle, which I found in the potting-shed and am having put in order for you. I hope little George— Lashmar, he will be too, won't he ?—will live to see his grandchildren cut their teeth on his mug.
                    Affectionately yours,
                            ALICE CONANT.

P.S.—How quiet you've kept about it all!

' Well, I'm——'
' Don't swear,' said Sophie. ' Bad for the infant mind.'
' But how in the world did she get at it ? Have you ever said a word about the Lashmars ? '
' You know the only time—to young Iggulden at Rocketts—when Iggulden died.'
' Your great-grandmother's brother ! She's traced the whole connection. More than your Aunt Sydney could do. What does she mean about our keeping quiet ? '
Sophie's eyes sparkled. ' I've thought that

out too. We've got back at the English at last.
Can't you see that *she* thought that *we* thought
my mother's being a Lashmar was one of those
things we'd expect the English to find out for
themselves, and that's impressed her?' She
turned the mug in her white hands, and sighed
happily. ' " Wayte awhyle—wayte awhyle."
That's not a bad motto, George. It's been worth
it.'

' But still I don't quite see——'

' I shouldn't wonder if they don't think our
coming here was part of a deep-laid scheme to be
near our ancestors. *They*'d understand that. And
look how they've accepted us, all of them.'

' Are we so undesirable in ourselves?' George
grunted.

' Be just, me lord. That wretched Sangres
man has twice our money. Can you see Marm
Conant slapping him between the shoulders?
Not by a jugful! The poor beast doesn't exist!'

' Do you think it's that then?' He looked
toward the cot by the fire where the godling
snorted.

' The minute I get well I shall find out from
Mrs. Cloke what every Lashmar gives in doles
(that's nicer than tips) every time a Lashmite is
born. I've done my duty thus far, but there's
much expected of me.'

Entered here Mrs. Cloke, and hung worship-
ping over the cot. They showed her the mug and
her face shone. ' Oh, now Lady Conant's sent it,
it'll be all proper, ma'am, won't it? " George "
of course he'd have to be, but seein' what he is

we was hopin'—all your people was hopin'—it
'ud be " Lashmar " too, and that 'ud just round
it out. A very 'andsome mug—quite unique, I
should imagine. "Wayte awhyle—wayte awhyle."
That's true with the Lashmars, I've heard. Very
slow to fill their houses, they are. Most like
Master George won't open 'is nursery till he's
thirty.'

' Poor lamb ! ' cried Sophie. ' But how did you
know my folk were Lashmars ? '

Mrs. Cloke thought deeply. ' I'm sure I can't
quite say, ma'am, but I've a belief likely that it
was something you may have let drop to young
Iggulden when you was at Rocketts. That *may*
have been what give us an inkling. An' so it
came out, one thing in the way o' talk leading to
another, and those American people at Veering
Holler was very obligin' with news, I'm told,
ma'am.'

' Great Scott ! ' said George, under his breath.
' And this is the simple peasant ! '

' Yiss,' Mrs. Cloke went on. ' An' Cloke was
only wonderin' this afternoon—your pillow's
slipped, my dear, you mustn't lie that a-way—just
for the sake o' sayin' something, whether you
wouldn't think well now of getting the Lashmar
farms back, sir. They don't rightly round off Sir
Walter's estate. They come caterin' across us
more. Cloke, 'e 'ud be glad to show you over
any day.'

' But Sir Walter doesn't want to sell, does he ? '

' We can find out from his bailiff, sir, but '—
with cold contempt—' I think that trained nurse

is just comin' up from her dinner, so I'm afraid we'll 'ave to ask you, sir . . . Now, Master George—Ai-ie! Wake a litty-minute, lammie!'

A few months later the three of them were down at the brook in the Gale Anstey woods to consider the rebuilding of a footbridge carried away by spring floods. George Lashmar wanted all the bluebells on God's earth that day to eat, and Sophie adored him in a voice like to the cooing of a dove; so business was delayed.

'Here's the place,' said his father at last among the water forget-me-nots. 'But where the deuce are the larch-poles, Cloke? I told you to have them down here ready.'

'We'll get 'em down *if* you say so,' Cloke answered, with a thrust of the underlip they both knew.

'But I *did* say so. What on earth have you brought that timber-tug here for? We aren't building a railway bridge. Why, in America, half-a-dozen two-by-four bits would be ample.'

'I don't know nothin' about that,' said Cloke. 'An' I've nothin' to say against larch—*if* you want to make a temp'ry job of it. I ain't 'ere to tell you what isn't so, sir; an' you can't say I ever come creepin' up on you, or tryin' to lead you farther in than you set out——'

A year ago George would have danced with impatience. Now he scraped a little mud off his old gaiters with his spud, and waited.

'All I say is that you can put up larch and make a temp'ry job of it; and by the time the young master's married it'll have to be done again. Now, I've brought down a couple of as sweet six-by-eight oak timbers as we've ever drawed. You put 'em in an' it's off your mind for good an' all. T'other way—I don't say it ain't right, I'm only just sayin' what I think—but t'other way, he'll no sooner be married than we'll 'ave it *all* to do again. You've no call to regard my words, but you can't get out of *that*.'

'No,' said George after a pause; 'I've been realising that for some time. Make it oak then. We can't get out of it.'

THE RECALL

I AM the land of their fathers,
    In me the virtue stays.
I will bring back my children
    After certain days.

Under their feet in the grasses
    My clinging magic runs.
They shall return as strangers,
    They shall remain as sons.

Over their heads in the branches
    Of their new-bought ancient trees,
I weave an incantation,
    And draw them to my knees.

Scent of smoke in the evening,
    Smell of rain in the night,
The hours, the days and the seasons,
    Order their souls aright ;

Till I make plain the meaning
    Of all my thousand years—
Till I fill their hearts with knowledge,
    While I fill their eyes with tears.

Garm—a Hostage

Garm—a Hostage

ONE night, a very long time ago, I drove to an Indian military cantonment called Mian Mir to see amateur theatricals. At the back of the Infantry barracks a soldier, his cap over one eye, rushed in front of the horses and shouted that he was a dangerous highway robber. As a matter of fact he was a friend of mine, so I told him to go home before any one caught him; but he fell under the pole, and I heard voices of a military guard in search of some one.

The driver and I coaxed him into the carriage, drove home swiftly, undressed him and put him to bed, where he waked next morning with a sore headache, very much ashamed. When his uniform was cleaned and dried, and he had been shaved and washed and made neat, I drove him back to barracks with his arm in a fine white sling, and reported that I had accidentally run over him. I did not tell this story to my friend's sergeant, who was a hostile and unbelieving person, but to his lieutenant, who did not know us quite so well.

Three days later my friend came to call, and at his heels slobbered and fawned one of the finest bull-terriers—of the old-fashioned breed, two parts bull and one terrier—that I had ever set eyes on. He was pure white, with a fawn-coloured saddle just behind his neck, and a fawn diamond at the root of his thin whippy tail. I had admired him distantly for more than a year; and Vixen, my own fox-terrier, knew him too, but did not approve.

' 'E's for you,' said my friend; but he did not look as though he liked parting with him.

' Nonsense! That dog's worth more than most men, Stanley,' I said.

' 'E's that an' more. 'Tention!'

The dog rose on his hind legs, and stood upright for a full minute.

' Eyes right!'

He sat on his haunches and turned his head sharp to the right. At a sign he rose and barked thrice. Then he shook hands with his right paw and bounded lightly to my shoulder. Here he made himself into a necktie, limp and lifeless, hanging down on either side of my neck. I was told to pick him up and throw him in the air. He fell with a howl, and held up one leg.

' Part o' the trick,' said his owner. ' You're going to die now. Dig yourself your little grave an' shut your little eye.'

Still limping, the dog hobbled to the garden-edge, dug a hole and lay down in it. When told that he was cured he jumped out, wagging his tail, and whining for applause. He was put through half-a-dozen other tricks, such as showing how he would hold a man safe (I was that man, and he sat down before me, his teeth bared, ready to spring), and how he would cease eating at the word of command. I had no more than finished praising him when my friend made a gesture that stopped the dog as though he had been shot, took a piece of blue-ruled canteen-paper from his helmet, handed it to me and ran away, while the dog looked after him and howled. I read:—

Sir—I give you the dog because of what you got me out of. He is the best I know, for I made him myself, and he is as good as a man. Please do not give him too much to eat, and please do not give him back to me, for I'm not going to take him, if you will keep him. So please do not try to give him back any more. I have kept his name back, so you can call him anything and he will answer, but please do not give him back. He can kill a man as easy as anything, but please do not give him too much meat. He knows more than a man.

Vixen sympathetically joined her shrill little yap to the bull-terrier's despairing cry, and I was annoyed, for I knew that a man who cares for dogs is one thing, but a man who loves one dog is quite another. Dogs are, at the best, no more than verminous vagrants, self-scratchers, foul feeders, and unclean by the law of Moses and Mohammed; but a dog with whom one lives alone for at least six months in the year; a free thing, tied to you so strictly by love that without you he will not stir or exercise; a patient, temperate, humorous, wise soul, who knows your moods before you know them yourself, is not a dog under any ruling.

E

I had Vixen, who was all my dog to me; and I felt what my friend must have felt, at tearing out his heart in this style and leaving it in my garden. However, the dog understood clearly enough that I was his master, and did not follow the soldier. As soon as he drew breath I made much of him, and Vixen, yelling with jealousy, flew at him. Had she been of his own sex, he might have cheered himself with a fight, but he only looked worriedly when she nipped his deep iron sides, laid his heavy head on my knee, and howled anew. I meant to dine at the Club that night, but as darkness drew in, and the dog snuffed through the empty house like a child trying to recover from a fit of sobbing, I felt that I could not leave him to suffer his first evening alone. So we fed at home, Vixen on one side and the stranger-dog on the other; she watching his every mouthful, and saying explicitly what she thought of his table manners, which were much better than hers.

It was Vixen's custom, till the weather grew hot, to sleep in my bed, her head on the pillow like a Christian; and when morning came I would always find that the little thing had braced her feet against the wall and pushed me to the very edge of the cot. This night she hurried to bed purposefully, every hair up and one eye on the stranger, who had dropped on a mat in a helpless, hopeless sort of way, his four feet spread out, sighing heavily. She settled her head on the pillow several times, to show her little airs and graces, and struck up her usual whiney sing-song before slumber. The stranger-dog softly edged towards me. I put out my hand and he licked it. Instantly my wrist was between Vixen's teeth, and her warning *aaarh!* said as plainly as speech that if I took any further notice of the stranger she would bite.

I caught her behind her fat neck with my left hand, shook her severely, and said:—

'Vixen, if you do that again you'll be put into the veranda. Now, remember!'

She understood perfectly, but the minute I released her she mouthed my right wrist once more, and waited with her ears back and all her body flattened, ready to bite. The big dog's tail thumped the floor in a humble and peace-making way.

I grabbed Vixen a second time, lifted her out of bed like a rabbit (she hated that and yelled), and, as I had promised, set her out in the veranda with the bats and the moonlight. At this she howled. Then she used coarse language—not to me, but to the bull-terrier—till she coughed with exhaustion. Then she ran round the house trying every door. Then she went off to the stables and barked as though some one were stealing the horses, which was an old trick of hers. Last she returned, and her snuffing yelp said, 'I'll be good! Let me in and I'll be good!'

She was admitted and flew to her pillow. When she was quieted I whispered to the other dog, 'You can lie on the foot of the bed.' The bull jumped up at once, and though I felt Vixen quiver with rage, she knew better than to protest.

So we slept till the morning, and they had early
breakfast with me, bite for bite, till the horse
came round and we went for a ride. I don't
think the bull had ever followed a horse before.
He was wild with excitement, and Vixen, as usual,
squealed and scuttered and scooted, and took
charge of the procession.

There was one corner of a village near by,
which we generally passed with caution, because
all the yellow pariah-dogs of the place gathered
about it. They were half-wild, starving beasts,
and though utter cowards, yet where nine or ten
of them get together they will mob and kill and
eat an English dog. I kept a whip with a long
lash for them. That morning they attacked
Vixen, who, perhaps of design, had moved from
beyond my horse's shadow.

The bull was ploughing along in the dust,
fifty yards behind, rolling in his run, and smiling
as bull-terriers will. I heard Vixen squeal. Half-
a-dozen of the curs closed in on her; a white
streak came up behind me; a cloud of dust rose
near Vixen, and, when it cleared, I saw one tall
pariah with his back broken, and the bull wrench-
ing another to earth. Vixen retreated to the pro-
tection of my whip, and the bull paddled back
smiling more than ever, covered with the blood
of his enemies. That decided me to call him
' Garm of the Bloody Breast,' who was a great
person in his time, or ' Garm ' for short; so,
leaning forward, I told him what his temporary
name would be. He looked up while I repeated
it, and then raced away. I shouted ' Garm ! ' He

stopped, raced back, and came up to ask my will.

Then I saw that my soldier-friend was right, and that that dog knew, and was worth, more than a man. At the end of the ride I gave an order which Vixen knew and hated: ' Go away and get washed!' I said. Garm understood some part of it, and Vixen interpreted the rest, and the two trotted off together soberly. When I went to the back veranda Vixen had been washed snowy-white, and was very proud of herself, but the dog-boy would not touch Garm on any account unless I stood by. So I waited while he was being scrubbed, and Garm, with the soap creaming on the top of his broad head, looked at me to make sure that this was what I expected him to endure. He knew perfectly that the dog-boy was only obeying orders.

' Another time,' I said to the dog-boy, ' you will wash the great dog with Vixen when I send them home.'

' Does *he* know? ' said the dog-boy, who understood the ways of dogs.

' Garm,' I said, ' another time you will be washed with Vixen.'

I knew that Garm understood. Indeed, next washing-day, when Vixen as usual fled under my bed, Garm stared at the doubtful dog-boy in the veranda, stalked to the place where he had been washed last time, and stood rigid in his tub.

But the long days in my office tried him sorely. We three would drive off in the morning at half-past eight and come home at six or later.

Vixen, knowing the routine of it, went to sleep under my table; but the confinement ate into Garm's soul. He generally sat on the veranda looking out on the Mall; and well I knew what he expected.

Sometimes a company of soldiers would move along on their way to the Fort, and Garm rolled forth to inspect them; or an officer in uniform entered into the office, and it was pitiful to see poor Garm's welcome to the cloth—not the man. He would leap at him, and sniff and bark joyously, then run to the door and back again. One afternoon I heard him bay with a full throat—a thing he had never done before—and he disappeared. When I drove into my garden at the end of the day a soldier in white uniform scrambled over the wall at the far end, and the Garm that met me was a joyous dog. This happened twice or thrice a week for a month.

I pretended not to notice, but Garm knew and Vixen knew. He would glide homewards from the office about four o'clock, as though he were only going to look at the scenery, and this he did so quietly that but for Vixen I should not have noticed him. The jealous little dog under the table would give a sniff and a snort, just loud enough to call my attention to the flight. Garm might go out forty times in the day and Vixen would never stir, but when he slunk off to see his true master in my garden she told me in her own tongue. That was the one sign she made to show that Garm did not altogether belong to the family. They were the best of friends at all times, *but*, Vixen explained that I was never to forget Garm did not love me as she loved me.

I never expected it. The dog was not my dog —could never be my dog—and I knew he was as miserable as his master who tramped eight miles a day to see him. So it seemed to me that the sooner the two were reunited the better for all. One afternoon I sent Vixen home alone in the dog-cart (Garm had gone before), and rode over to cantonments to find another friend of mine, who was an Irish soldier and a great friend of the dog's master.

I explained the whole case, and wound up with:

' And now Stanley's in my garden crying over his dog. Why doesn't he take him back? They're both unhappy.'

' Unhappy! There's no sense in the little man any more. But 'tis his fit.'

' What *is* his fit? He travels fifty miles a week to see the brute, and he pretends not to notice me when he sees me on the road; and I'm as unhappy as he is. Make him take the dog back.'

' It's his penance he's set himself. I told him by way av a joke, afther you'd run over him so convenient that night, whin he was dhrunk—I said if he was a Catholic he'd do penance. Off he went wid that fit in his little head *an'* a dose av fever, an' nothin' would suit but givin' you the dog as a hostage.'

' Hostage for what? I don't want hostages from Stanley.'

' For his good behaviour. He's keepin' straight now, the way it's no pleasure to associate wid him.'

' Has he taken the pledge? '

' If 'twas only *that* I need not care. Ye can take the pledge for three months on an' off. He sez he'll never see the dog again, an' *so*, mark you, he'll keep straight for evermore. Ye know his fits? Well, this is wan av them. How's the dog takin' it? '

' Like a man. He's the best dog in India. Can't you make Stanley take him back? '

' I can do no more than I have done. But ye know his fits. He's just doin' his penance. What will he do when he goes to the Hills? The docthor's put him on the list.'

It is the custom in India to send a certain number of invalids from each regiment up to stations in the Himalayas for the hot weather; and though the men ought to enjoy the cool and the comfort, they miss the society of the barracks down below, and do their best to come back or to avoid going. I felt that this move would bring matters to a head, so I left Terence hopefully, though he called after me :—

' He won't take the dog, sorr. You can lay your month's pay on that. Ye know his fits.'

I never pretended to understand Private Ortheris ; and so I did the next best thing—I left him alone.

That summer the invalids of the regiment to which my friend belonged were ordered off to the Hills early, because the doctors thought marching in the cool of the day would do them good. Their route lay south to a place called Umballa, a hundred and twenty miles or more. Then they would

turn east and march up into the hills to Kasauli
or Dugshai or Subathoo. I dined with the officers
the night before they left—they were marching
at five in the morning. It was midnight when I
drove into my garden and surprised a white
figure flying over the wall.

'That man,' said my butler, 'has been here
since nine, making talk to that dog. He is quite
mad. I did not tell him to go away because he
has been here many times before, and because
the dog-boy told me that if I told him to go away,
that great dog would immediately slay me. He
did not wish to speak to the Protector of the Poor,
and he did not ask for anything to eat or drink.'

'Kadir Buksh,' said I, 'that was well done,
for the dog would surely have killed thee. But I
do not think the white soldier will come any
more.'

Garm slept ill that night and whimpered in his
dreams. Once he sprang up with a clear, ringing
bark, and I heard him wag his tail till it waked
him and the bark died out in a howl. He had
dreamed he was with his master again, and I
nearly cried. It was all Stanley's silly fault.

The first halt which the detachment of invalids
made was some miles from their barracks, on the
Amritzar road, and ten miles distant from my
house. By a mere chance one of the officers drove
back for another good dinner at the Club (cooking
on the line of march is always bad), and there I
met him. He was a particular friend of mine,
and I knew that he knew how to love a dog
properly. His pet was a big fat retriever who

was going up to the Hills for his health, and, though it was still April, the round brown brute puffed and panted in the Club veranda as though he would burst.

' It's amazing,' said the officer, ' what excuses these invalids of mine make to get back to barracks. There's a man in my company now asked me for leave to go back to cantonments to pay a debt he'd forgotten. I was so taken by the idea I let him go, and he jingled off in an *ekka* as pleased as Punch. Ten miles to pay a debt! Wonder what it was really?'

' If you'll drive me home I think I can show you,' I said.

So we went over to my house in his dog-cart with the retriever; and on the way I told him the story of Garm.

' I was wondering where that brute had gone to. He's the best dog in the regiment,' said my friend. ' I offered the little fellow twenty rupees for him a month ago. But he's a hostage, you say, for Stanley's good conduct. Stanley's one of the best men I have—when he chooses.'

' That's the reason why,' I said. ' A second-rate man wouldn't have taken things to heart as he has done.'

We drove in quietly at the far end of the garden, and crept round the house. There was a place close to the wall all grown about with tamarisk trees, where I knew Garm kept his bones. Even Vixen was not allowed to sit near it. In the full Indian moonlight I could see a white uniform bending over the dog.

' Good-bye, old man.' We could not help hearing Stanley's voice. ' For 'Eving's sake don't get bit and go mad by any measly pi-dog. But you can look after yourself, old man. *You* don't get drunk an' run about 'ittin' your friends. You takes your bones an' you eats your biscuit, an' you kills your enemy like a gentleman. I'm goin' away—don't 'owl—I'm goin' off to Kasauli where I won't see you no more.'

I could hear him holding Garm's nose as the dog threw it up to the stars.

' You'll stay here an' be'ave, an'—an' I'll go away an' try to be'ave, an' I don't know 'ow to leave you. I don't know——'

' I think this is damn' silly,' said the officer, patting his foolish fubsy old retriever. He called to the private, who leaped to his feet, marched forward, and saluted.

' You here?' said the officer, turning away his head.

' Yes, sir, but I'm just goin' back.'

' I shall be leaving here at eleven in my cart. You come with me. I can't have sick men running about all over the place. Report yourself at eleven, *here*.'

We did not say much when we went indoors, but the officer muttered and pulled his retriever's ears.

He was a disgraceful, overfed door-mat of a dog; and when he waddled off to my cookhouse to be fed, I had a brilliant idea.

At eleven o'clock that officer's dog was no-where to be found, and you never heard such a fuss

as his owner made. He called and shouted and
grew angry, and hunted through my garden for
half an hour.

Then I said :—

'He's sure to turn up in the morning. Send
a man in by rail, and I'll find the beast and return
him.'

'Beast?' said the officer. 'I value that dog
considerably more than I value any man I know.
It's all very fine for you to talk. Your dog's here.'

So she was—under my feet—and, had she
been missing, food and wages would have stopped
in my house till her return. But some people
grow fond of dogs not worth a cut of the whip.
My friend had to drive away at last with Stanley
in the back-seat. And then the dog-boy said to
me :—

'What kind of animal is Bullen Sahib's dog?
Look at him !'

I went to the boy's hut, and the fat old re-
probate was lying on a mat carefully chained
up. He must have heard his master calling for
twenty minutes, but had not even attempted to
join him.

'He has no face,' said the dog-boy scornfully.
'He is a *punniar-kooter* [a spaniel]. He never
tried to get that cloth off his jaws when his master
called. Now Vixen-*baba* would have jumped
through the window, and the Great Dog would
have slain me with his muzzled mouth. It is true
that there are many kinds of dogs.'

Next evening who should turn up but Stanley.
The officer had sent him back fourteen miles by

rail with a note begging me to return the retriever if I had found him, and, if I had not, to offer huge rewards. The last train to camp left at half-past ten, and Stanley stayed till ten talking to Garm. I argued and entreated, and even threatened to shoot the bull-terrier, but the little man was as firm as a rock, though I gave him a good dinner and talked to him most severely. Garm knew as well as I that this was the last time he could hope to see his man, and followed Stanley like a shadow. The retriever said nothing, but licked his lips after his meal and waddled off without so much as saying ' Thank you ' to the disgusted dog-boy.

So that last meeting was over and I felt as wretched as Garm, who moaned in his sleep all night. When we went to the office he found a place under the table close to Vixen, and dropped flat till it was time to go home. There was no more running out into the verandas, no slinking away for stolen talks with Stanley. As the weather grew warmer the dogs were forbidden to run beside the cart, but sat at my side on the seat, Vixen with her head under the crook of my left elbow, and Garm hugging the handrail.

Here Vixen was ever in great form. She had to attend to all the moving traffic, such as bullock-carts that blocked the way, and camels, and led ponies; as well as to keep up her dignity when she passed low friends running in the dust. She never yapped for yapping's sake, but her shrill, high bark was known all along the Mall, and other men's terriers ki-yied in reply, and bullock-

drivers looked over their shoulders and gave us
the road with a grin.

But Garm cared for none of these things. His
big eyes were on the horizon and his terrible
mouth was shut. There was another dog in the
office who belonged to my Chief. We called him
' Bob the Librarian,' because he always imagined
vain rats behind the bookshelves, and in hunting
for them would drag out half the old newspaper-
files. Bob was a well-meaning idiot, but Garm did
not encourage him. He would slide his head
round the door, panting, ' Rats ! Come along,
Garm !' and Garm would shift one fore-paw over
the other, and curl himself round, leaving Bob to
whine at a most uninterested back. The office
was nearly as cheerful as a tomb in those days.

Once, and only once, did I see Garm at all
contented with his surroundings. He had gone
for an unauthorised walk with Vixen early one
Sunday morning, and a very young and foolish
artilleryman (his battery had just moved to that
part of the world) tried to steal them both. Vixen,
of course, knew better than to take food from
soldiers, and, besides, she had just finished her
breakfast. So she trotted back with a large piece
of the mutton that they issue to our troops, laid
it down on my veranda, and looked up to see what
I thought. I asked her where Garm was, and she
ran in front of the horse to show me the way.

About a mile up the road we came across our
artilleryman sitting very stiffly on the edge of a
culvert with a greasy handkerchief on his knees.
Garm was in front of him, looking rather pleased.

When the man moved leg or hand, Garm bared his teeth in silence. A broken string hung from his collar, and the other half of it lay, all warm, in the artilleryman's still hand. He explained to me, keeping his eyes straight in front of him, that he had met this dog (he called him awful names) walking alone, and was going to take him to the Fort to be killed for a masterless pariah.

I said that Garm did not seem to me much of a pariah, but that he had better take him to the Fort if he thought best. He said he did not care to do so. I told him to go to the Fort alone. He said he did not want to go at that hour, but would follow my advice as soon as I had called off the dog. I instructed Garm to take him to the Fort, and Garm marched him solemnly up to the gate, one mile and a half under a hot sun, and I told the quarter-guard what had happened; but the young artilleryman was more angry than was at all necessary when they began to laugh. Several regiments, he was told, had tried to steal Garm in their time.

That month the hot weather shut down in earnest, and the dogs slept in the bathroom on the cool wet bricks where the bath is placed. Every morning, as soon as the man filled my bath, the two jumped in, and every morning the man filled the bath a second time. I said to him that he might as well fill a small tub specially for the dogs. 'Nay,' said he, smiling, 'it is not their custom. They would not understand. Besides, the big bath gives them more space.'

The punkah-coolies who pull the punkahs day

and night came to know Garm intimately. He
noticed that when the swaying fan stopped I
would call out to the coolie and bid him pull with
a long stroke. If the man still slept I would wake
him up. He discovered, too, that it was a good
thing to lie in the wave of air under the punkah.
Maybe Stanley had taught him all about this
in barracks. At any rate, when the punkah
stopped, Garm would first growl and cock his
eye at the rope, and if that did not wake the man—
it nearly always did—he would tiptoe forth and
talk in the sleeper's ear. Vixen was a clever little
dog, but she could never connect the punkah
and the coolie; so Garm gave me grateful hours
of cool sleep. But he was utterly wretched—as
miserable as a human being; and in his misery
he clung so closely to me that other men noticed
it and were envious. If I moved from one room
to another Garm followed; if my pen stopped
scratching, Garm's head was thrust into my
hand; if I turned, half awake, on the pillow,
Garm was up and at my side, for he knew that I
was his only link with his master, and day and
night, and night and day, his eyes asked one
question—' When is this going to end?'

Living with the dog as I did, I never noticed
that he was more than ordinarily upset by the hot
weather, till one day at the Club a man said:
' That dog of yours will die in a week or two. He's
a shadow.' Then I dosed Garm with iron and
quinine, which he hated; and I felt very anxious.
He lost his appetite, and Vixen was allowed to
eat his dinner under his eyes. Even that did not

make him swallow, and we held a consultation on him, of the best man-doctor in the place; a lady-doctor, who cured the sick wives of kings; and the Deputy Inspector-General of the veterinary service of all India. They pronounced upon his symptoms, and I told them his story, and Garm lay on a sofa licking my hand.

' He's dying of a broken heart,' said the lady-doctor suddenly.

' 'Pon my word,' said the Deputy Inspector-General, ' I believe Mrs. Macrae is perfectly right—as usual.'

The best man-doctor in the place wrote a prescription, and the veterinary Deputy Inspector-General went over it afterwards to be sure that the drugs were in the proper dog-proportions; and that was the first time in his life that our doctor ever allowed his prescriptions to be edited. It was a strong tonic, and it put the old boy on his feet for a week or two; then he lost flesh again. I asked a man I knew to take him up to the Hills with him when he went, and the man came to the door with his kit packed on the top of the carriage. Garm took in the situation at one red glance. The hair rose along his back; he sat down in front of me and delivered the most awful growl I have ever heard in the jaws of a dog. I shouted to my friend to get away at once, and as soon as the carriage was out of the garden Garm laid his head on my knee and whined. So I knew his answer, and devoted myself to getting Stanley's address in the Hills.

My turn to go to the cool came late in August.

F

We were allowed thirty days' holiday in a year, if no one fell sick, and we took it as we could be spared. My Chief and Bob the Librarian had their holiday first, and when they were gone I made a calendar, as I always did, and hung it up at the head of my cot, tearing off one day at a time till they returned. Vixen had gone up to the Hills with me five times before; and she appreciated the cold and the damp and the beautiful wood fires there as much as I did.

'Garm,' I said, 'we are going back to Stanley at Kasauli. Kasauli—Stanley; Stanley—Kasauli.' And I repeated it twenty times. It was not Kasauli really, but another place. Still I remembered what Stanley had said in my garden on the last night, and I dared not change the name. Then Garm began to tremble; then he barked; and then he leaped up at me, frisking and wagging his tail.

'Not now,' I said, holding up my hand. 'When I say " Go," we'll go, Garm.' I pulled out the little blanket coat and spiked collar that Vixen always wore up in the Hills, to protect her against sudden chills and thieving leopards, and I let the two smell them and talk it over. What they said of course I do not know, but it made a new dog of Garm. His eyes were bright; and he barked joyfully when I spoke to him. He ate his food, and he killed his rats for the next three weeks, and when he began to whine I had only to say ' Stanley—Kasauli; Kasauli—Stanley,' to wake him up. I wish I had thought of it before.

My Chief came back, all brown with living in the open air, and very angry at finding it so hot in the Plains. That same afternoon we three and Kadir Buksh began to pack for our month's holiday, Vixen rolling in and out of the bullock-trunk twenty times a minute, and Garm grinning all over and thumping on the floor with his tail. Vixen knew the routine of travelling as well as she knew my office-work. She went to the station, singing songs, on the front seat of the carriage, while Garm sat with me. She hurried into the railway carriage, saw Kadir Buksh make up my bed for the night, got her drink of water, and curled up with her black-patch eye on the tumult of the platform. Garm followed her (the crowd gave him a lane all to himself) and sat down on the pillows with his eyes blazing, and his tail a haze behind him.

We came to Umballa in the hot misty dawn, four or five men, who had been working hard for eleven months, shouting for our dâks—the two-horse travelling carriages that were to take us up to Kalka at the foot of the Hills. It was all new to Garm. He did not understand carriages where you lay at full length on your bedding, but Vixen knew and hopped into her place at once; Garm following. The Kalka Road, before the railway was built, was about forty-seven miles long, and the horses were changed every eight miles. Most of them jibbed, and kicked, and plunged, but they had to go, and they went rather better than usual for Garm's deep bay in their rear.

There was a river to be forded, and four

bullocks pulled the carriage, and Vixen stuck her head out of the sliding-door and nearly fell into the water while she gave directions. Garm was silent and curious, and rather needed reassuring about Stanley and Kasauli. So we rolled, barking and yelping, into Kalka for lunch, and Garm ate enough for two.

After Kalka the road wound among the hills, and we took a curricle with half-broken ponies, which were changed every six miles. No one dreamed of a railroad to Simla in those days, for it was seven thousand feet up in the air. The road was more than fifty miles long, and the regulation pace was just as fast as the ponies could go. Here, again, Vixen led Garm from one carriage to the other, jumped into the back seat, and shouted. A cool breath from the snows met us about five miles out of Kalka, and she whined for her coat, wisely fearing a chill on the liver. I had had one made for Garm too, and, as we climbed to the fresh breezes, I put it on, and Garm chewed it uncomprehendingly, but I think he was grateful.

'Hi-yi-yi-yi!' sang Vixen as we shot round the curves; 'Toot-toot-toot!' went the driver's bugle at the dangerous places, and 'Yow! yow! yow!' bayed Garm. Kadir Buksh sat on the front seat and smiled. Even he was glad to get away from the heat of the Plains that stewed in the haze behind us. Now and then we would meet a man we knew going down to his work again, and he would say: 'What's it like below?' and I would shout: 'Hotter than cinders. What's it like up above?' and he would shout back: ' Just perfect! ' and away we would go.

Suddenly Kadir Buksh said, over his shoulder:
' Here is Solon '; and Garm snored where he lay
with his head on my knee. Solon is an unpleasant
little cantonment, but it has the advantage of being
cool and healthy. It is all bare and windy, and
one generally stops at a rest-house near by for
something to eat. I got out and took both dogs
with me, while Kadir Buksh made tea. A soldier
told us we should find Stanley ' out there,' nodding
his head towards a bare, bleak hill.

When we climbed to the top we spied that
very Stanley, who had given me all this trouble,
sitting on a rock with his face in his hands and his
overcoat hanging loose about him. I never saw
anything so lonely and dejected in my life as this
one little man, crumpled up and thinking, on the
great grey hillside.

Here Garm left me.

He departed without a word, and, so far as
I could see, without moving his legs. He flew
through the air bodily, and I heard the whack of
him as he flung himself at Stanley, knocking the
little man clean over. They rolled on the ground
together, shouting, and yelping, and hugging. I
could not see which was dog and which was man,
till Stanley got up and whimpered.

He told me that he had been suffering from
fever at intervals, and was very weak. He looked
all he said, but even while I watched, both man
and dog plumped out to their natural sizes,
precisely as dried apples swell in water. Garm
was on his shoulder and his breast and feet all at

the same time, so that Stanley spoke all through a cloud of Garm—gulping, sobbing, slavering Garm. He did not say anything that I could understand, except that he had fancied he was going to die, but that now he was quite well, and that he was not going to give up Garm any more to anybody under the rank of Beelzebub.

Then he said he felt hungry, and thirsty, and happy.

We went down to tea at the rest-house, where Stanley stuffed himself with sardines and raspberry jam, and beer, and cold mutton and pickles, when Garm wasn't climbing over him; and then Vixen and I went on.

Garm saw how it was at once. He said good-bye to me three times, giving me both paws one after another, and leaping on to my shoulder. He further escorted us, singing Hosannas at the top of his voice, a mile down the road. Then he raced back to his own master.

Vixen never opened her mouth, but when the cold twilight came, and we could see the lights of Simla across the hills, she snuffled with her nose at the breast of my ulster. I unbuttoned it, and tucked her inside. Then she gave a contented little sniff, and fell fast asleep, her head on my breast, till we bundled out at Simla, two of the four happiest people in all the world that night.

THE POWER OF THE DOG

THERE is sorrow enough in the natural way
From men and women to fill our day;
But when we are certain of sorrow in store,
Why do we always arrange for more?
Brothers and sisters, I bid you beware
Of giving your heart to a dog to tear.

Buy a pup and your money will buy
Love unflinching that cannot lie—
Perfect passion and worship fed
By a kick in the ribs or a pat on the head.
Nevertheless it is hardly fair
To risk your heart for a dog to tear.

When the fourteen years which Nature permits
Are closing in asthma, or tumour, or fits,
And the Vet's unspoken prescription runs
To lethal chambers or loaded guns,
Then you will find—it's your own affair,
But . . . you've given your heart to a dog to tear.

When the body that lived at your single will,
With its whimper of welcome, is stilled (how still!),
When the spirit that answered your every mood
Is gone—wherever it goes—for good,
You will discover how much you care,
And will give your heart to a dog to tear!

We've sorrow enough in the natural way,
When it comes to burying Christian clay.
Our loves are not given, but only lent,
At compound interest of cent per cent.
Though it is not always the case, I believe,
That the longer we've kept 'em, the more do we grieve;
For, when debts are payable, right or wrong,
A short-time loan is as bad as a long—
So why in—Heaven (before we are there)
Should we give our hearts to a dog to tear?

The Mother Hive

The Mother Hive

IF the stock had not been old and overcrowded, the Wax-moth would never have entered; but where bees are too thick on the comb there must be sickness or parasites. The heat of the hive had risen with the June honey-flow, and though the fanners worked until their wings ached, to keep people cool, everybody suffered.

A young bee crawled up the greasy, trampled alighting-board. 'Excuse me,' she began, 'but it's my first honey-flight. Could you kindly tell me if this is my——'

'——own hive?' the Guard snapped. 'Yes! Buzz in, and be foul-brooded to you! Next!'

'Shame!' cried half-a-dozen old workers with worn wings and nerves, and there was a scuffle and a hum.

The little grey Wax-moth, pressed close in a crack in the alighting-board, had waited this chance all day. She scuttled in like a ghost, and, knowing the senior bees would turn her out at once, dodged into a brood-frame, where youngsters who had not yet seen the winds blow or the flowers nod discussed life. Here she was safe, for young bees will tolerate any sort of stranger. Behind her came the bee who had been slanged by the Guard.

'What is the world like, Melissa?' said a companion.

'Cruel! I brought in a full load of first-class stuff, and the Guard told me to go and be foul-brooded!' She sat down in the cool draught across the combs.

'If you'd only heard,' said the Wax-moth silkily, 'the insolence of the Guard's tone when she cursed our sister! It aroused the Entire Community.' She laid an egg. She had stolen in for that purpose.

'There *was* a bit of a fuss on the Gate,' Melissa chuckled. 'You were there, Miss——?' She did not know how to address the slim stranger.

'Don't call me "Miss." I'm a sister to all in affliction—just a working sister. My heart bled for you beneath your burden.' The Wax-moth caressed Melissa with her soft feelers and laid another egg.

'You mustn't lay here,' cried Melissa. 'You aren't a Queen.'

'My dear child, I give you my most solemn word of honour those aren't eggs. Those are my principles, and I am ready to die for them.' She raised her voice a little above the rustle and tramp round her. 'If you'd like to kill me, pray do.'

'Don't be unkind, Melissa,' said a young bee, impressed by the chaste folds of the Wax-moth's wing, which hid her ceaseless egg-dropping.

'*I* haven't done anything,' Melissa answered. 'She's doing it all.'

' Ah, don't let your conscience reproach you later, but when you've killed me, write me, at least, as one that loved her fellow-workers.'

Laying at every sob, the Wax-moth backed into a crowd of young bees, and left Melissa bewildered and annoyed. So she lifted up her little voice in the darkness and cried, ' Stores ! ' till a gang of cell-fillers hailed her, and she left her load with them.

' I'm afraid I foul-brooded you just now,' said a voice over her shoulder. ' I'd been on the Gate for three hours, and one would foul-brood the Queen herself after that. No offence meant.'

' None taken,' Melissa answered cheerily. ' I shall be on guard myself, some day. What's next to do ? '

' There's a rumour of Death's Head Moths about. Send a gang of youngsters to the Gate, and tell them to narrow it in with a couple of stout scrap-wax pillars. It'll make the Hive hot, but we can't have Death's Headers in the middle of the honey-flow.'

' My Only Wings ! I should think not ! ' Melissa had all a sound bee's hereditary hatred against the big, squeaking, feathery Thief of the Hives. ' Tumble out ! ' she called across the youngsters' quarters. ' All you who aren't feeding babies, show a leg. Scrap-wax pillars for the Ga-ate ! ' She chanted the order at length.

' That's nonsense,' a downy, day-old bee answered. ' In the first place, *I* never heard of a Death's Header coming into a hive. People don't *do* such things. In the second, building pillars to keep 'em out is purely a Cypriote trick, unworthy of British bees. In the third, if you trust a Death's Head, he will trust you. Pillar-building shows lack of confidence. Our dear sister in grey says so.'

' Yes. Pillars are un-English and provocative, and a waste of wax that is needed for higher and more practical ends,' said the Wax-moth from an empty store-cell.

' The safety of the Hive is the highest thing I've ever heard of. You mustn't teach us to refuse work,' Melissa began.

' You misunderstand me as usual, love. Work's the essence of life; but to expend precious unreturning vitality and real labour against imaginary danger, *that* is heartbreakingly absurd! If I can only teach a—a little toleration —a little ordinary kindness here towards that absurd old bogey you call the Death's Header, I shan't have lived in vain.'

' She *hasn't* lived in vain, the darling!' cried twenty bees together. ' You should see her saintly life, Melissa! She just devotes herself to spreading her principles, and—and—she looks lovely!'

An old, baldish bee came up the comb.

' Pillar-workers for the Gate! Get out and chew scraps. Buzz off!' she said. The Wax-moth slipped aside.

The young bees trooped down the frame, whispering.

' What's the matter with 'em?' said the oldster. ' Why do they call each other " ducky " and " darling "? Must be the weather.' She sniffed suspiciously. 'Horrid stuffy smell here. Like stale quilts. Not Wax-moth, I hope, Melissa?'

'Not to my knowledge,' said Melissa, who, of course, only knew the Wax-moth as a lady with principles, and had never thought to report her presence. She had always imagined Wax-moths to be like blood-red dragon-flies.

'You had better fan out this corner for a little,' said the old bee and passed on. Melissa dropped her head at once, took firm hold with her fore-feet, and fanned obediently at the regulation stroke—three hundred beats to the second. Fanning tries a bee's temper, because she must always keep in the same place where she never seems to be doing any good, and, all the while, she is wearing out her only wings. When a bee cannot fly, a bee must not live; and a bee knows it. The Wax-moth crept forth, and caressed Melissa again.

'I see,' she murmured, 'that at heart you are one of Us.'

'I work with the Hive,' Melissa answered briefly.

'It's the same thing. We and the Hive are one.'

'Then why are your feelers different from ours? Don't cuddle so.'

'Don't be provincial, *carissima*. You can't have all the world alike—yet.'

'But why do you lay eggs?' Melissa insisted. 'You lay 'em like a Queen—only you drop them in patches all over the place. I've watched you.'

'Ah, Brighteyes, so you've pierced my little

subterfuge? Yes, they *are* eggs. By and by they'll spread our principles. Aren't you glad?'

'You gave me your most solemn word of honour that they were not eggs.'

'That was my little subterfuge, dearest—for the sake of the Cause. Now I must reach the young.' The Wax-moth tripped towards the fourth brood-frame, where the young bees were busy feeding the babies.

It takes some time for a sound bee to realise a malignant and continuous lie. 'She's very sweet and feathery,' was all that Melissa thought, 'but her talk sounds like ivy honey tastes. I'd better get to my field-work again.'

She found the Gate in a sulky uproar. The youngsters told off to the pillars had refused to chew scrap-wax because it made their jaws ache, and were clamouring for virgin stuff.

'Anything to finish the job!' said the badgered Guards. 'Hang up, some of you, and make wax for these slack-jawed sisters.'

Before a bee can make wax she must fill herself with honey. Then she climbs to safe foothold and hangs, while other gorged bees hang on to her in a cluster. There they wait in silence till the wax comes. The scales are either taken out of the makers' pockets by the workers, or tinkle down on the workers while they wait. The workers chew them (they are useless unchewed) into the all-supporting, all-embracing Wax of the Hive.

But now, no sooner was the wax-cluster in position than the workers below broke out again.

' Come down ! ' they cried. ' Come down and work! Come on, you Levantine parasites! Don't think to enjoy yourselves up there while we're sweating down here ! '

The cluster shivered, as from hooked forefoot to hooked hind-foot it telegraphed uneasiness. At last a worker sprang up, grapped the lowest wax-maker, and swung, kicking, above her companions.

' I can make wax too ! ' she bawled. ' Give me a full gorge and I'll make tons of it.'

' Make it, then,' said the bee she had grappled. The spoken word snapped the current through the cluster. It shook and glistened like a cat's fur in the dark. ' Unhook ! ' it murmured. ' No wax for any one to-day.'

' You lazy thieves ! Hang up at once and produce our wax,' said the bees below.

' Impossible ! The sweat's gone. To make your wax we must have stillness, warmth, and food. Unhook ! Unhook ! '

They broke up as they murmured, and disappeared among the other bees, from whom, of course, they were undistinguishable.

' Seems as if we'd have to chew scrap-wax for these pillars, after all,' said a worker.

' Not by a whole comb,' cried the young bee who had broken the cluster. ' Listen here ! I've studied the question more than twenty minutes. It's as simple as falling off a daisy. You've heard of Cheshire, Root, and Langstroth ? '

They had not, but they shouted ' Good old Langstroth ! ' just the same.

G

'Those three know all that there is to be known about making hives. One or t'other of 'em must have made ours, and if they've made it, they're bound to look after it. Ours is a " Guaranteed Patent Hive." You can see it on the label behind.'

'Good old guarantee! Hurrah for the label behind!' roared the bees.

'Well, such being the case, *I* say that when we find they've betrayed us, we can exact from them a terrible vengeance.'

'Good old vengeance! Good old Root! 'Nuff said! Chuck it!' The crowd cheered and broke away as Melissa dived through.

'D'you know where Langstroth, Root, and Cheshire live if you happen to want 'em?' she asked of the proud and panting orator.

'Gum me if I know they ever lived at all! But aren't they beautiful names to buzz about? Did you see how it worked up the sisterhood?'

'Yes, but it didn't defend the Gate,' she replied.

'Ah, perhaps that's true, but think how delicate *my* position is, sister. I've a magnificent appetite, and I don't like working. It's bad for the mind. My instinct tells me that I can act as a restraining influence on others. They would have been worse, but for me.'

But Melissa had already risen clear, and was heading for a breadth of virgin white clover, which to an over-tired bee is as soothing as plain knitting to a woman.

'I think I'll take this load to the nurseries,'

she said, when she had finished. ' It was always quiet there in my day,' and she topped off with two little pats of pollen for the babies.

She was met on the fourth brood-comb by a rush of excited sisters all buzzing together.

' One at a time! Let me put down my load. Now, what is it, Sacharissa?' she said.

' Grey Sister—that fluffy one, I mean—she came and said we ought to be out in the sunshine gathering honey, because life was short. She said any old bee could attend to our babies, and some day old bees would. That isn't true, Melissa, is it? No old bees can take us away from our babies, can they?'

' Of course not. You feed the babies while your heads are soft. When your heads harden, you go on to field-work. Any one knows that.'

' We told her so. We *told* her so! But she only waved her feelers, and said we could all lay eggs like Queens if we chose. And I'm afraid lots of the weaker sisters believe her, and are trying to do it. *So* unsettling!'

Sacharissa sped to a sealed worker-cell whose lid pulsated, as the bee within began to cut its way out.

' Come along, precious!' she murmured, and thinned the frail top from the other side. A pale, damp, creased thing hoisted itself feebly on to the comb. Sacharissa's note changed at once. ' No time to waste! Go up the frame and preen yourself!' she said. ' Report for nursing-duty in my ward to-morrow evening at six. Stop a minute. What's the matter with your third right leg?'

The young bee held it out in silence—
unmistakably a drone leg incapable of packing
pollen.

'Thank you. You needn't report till the day
after to-morrow.' Sacharissa turned to her companion. 'That's the fifth oddity hatched in my
ward since noon. I don't like it.'

'There's always a certain number of 'em,'
said Melissa. 'You can't stop a few working
sisters from laying, now and then, when they
overfeed themselves. They only raise dwarf
drones.'

'But we're hatching out drones with workers'
stomachs; workers with drones' stomachs; and
albinos and mixed-leggers who can't pack pollen—
like that poor little beast yonder. I don't mind
dwarf drones any more than you do (they all die
in July), but this steady hatch of oddities frightens
me, Melissa!'

'How narrow of you! They are all so de-
lightfully clever and unusual and interesting,'
piped the Wax-moth from a crack above them.
'Come here, you dear, downy duck, and tell us
all about your feelings.'

'I wish she'd go!' Sacharissa lowered her
voice. 'She meets these—er—oddities as they
dry out, and cuddles 'em in corners.'

'I suppose the truth is that we're over-
stocked and too well fed to swarm,' said Melissa.

'That *is* the truth,' said the Queen's voice
behind them. They had not heard the heavy
royal footfall which sets empty cells vibrating.
Sacharissa offered her food at once. She ate

and dragged her weary body forward. ' Can you suggest a remedy? ' she said.

'New principles! ' cried the Wax-moth from her crevice. ' We'll apply them quietly—later.'

' Suppose we sent out a swarm? ' Melissa suggested. ' It's a little late, but it might ease us off.'

' It would save us, but—I know the Hive! You shall see for yourself.' The old Queen cried the Swarming Cry, which to a bee of good blood should be what the trumpet was to Job's warhorse. In spite of her immense age (three years), it rang between the cañon-like frames as a pibroch rings in a mountain pass; the fanners changed their note, and repeated it up in every gallery; and the broad-winged drones, burly and eager, ended it on one nerve-thrilling outbreak of bugles: '*La Reine le veult! Swarm! Swar-rm! Swar-r-rm!* '

But the roar which should follow the Call was wanting. They heard a broken grumble like the murmur of a falling tide.

' Swarm? What for? Catch me leaving a good bar-frame Hive, with fixed foundations, for a rotten old oak out in the open where it may rain any minute! *We*'re all right! It's a " Patent Guaranteed Hive." Why do they want to turn us out? Swarming be gummed! Swarming was invented to cheat a worker out of her proper comforts. Come on off to bed! '

The noise died out as the bees settled in empty cells for the night.

' You hear? ' said the Queen. ' I know the Hive! '

' Quite between ourselves, *I* taught them that,' cried the Wax-moth. ' Wait till my principles develop, and you'll see the light from a new quarter.'

' You speak truth for once,' the Queen said suddenly, for she recognised the Wax-moth. ' That Light will break into the top of the Hive. A Hot Smoke will follow it, and your children will not be able to hide in any crevice.'

' Is it possible? ' Melissa whispered. ' I—we have sometimes heard a legend like it.'

' It is no legend,' the old Queen answered. ' I had it from my mother, and she had it from hers. After the Wax-moth has grown strong, a Shadow will fall across the Gate ; a Voice will speak from behind a Veil ; there will be Light, and Hot Smoke, and earthquakes, and those who live will see everything that they have done, all together in one place, burned up in one great Fire.' The old Queen was trying to tell what she had been told of the Bee Master's dealings with an infected hive in the apiary, two or three seasons ago ; and, of course, from her point of view the affair was as important as the Day of Judgment.

' And then? ' asked horrified Sacharissa.

' Then, I have heard that a little light will burn in a great darkness, and perhaps the world will begin again. Myself, I think not.'

' Tut ! Tut ! ' the Wax-moth cried. ' You good, fat people always prophesy ruin if things don't go exactly your way. But I grant you there will be changes.'

There were. When her eggs hatched, the

wax was riddled with little tunnels, coated with the
dirty clothes of the caterpillars. Flannelly lines
ran through the honey-stores, the pollen-larders,
the foundations, and, worst of all, through the
babies in their cradles, till the Sweeper Guards
spent half their time tossing out useless little
corpses. The lines ended in a maze of sticky
webbing on the face of the comb. The caterpillars could not stop spinning as they walked,
and as they walked everywhere, they smarmed
and garmed everything. Even where it did not
hamper the bees' feet, the stale, sour smell of the
stuff put them off their work ; though some of the
bees who had taken to egg-laying said it encouraged
them to be mothers and maintain a vital interest in
life.

When the caterpillars became moths, they
made friends with the ever-increasing Oddities—
albinos, mixed-leggers, single-eyed composites,
faceless drones, half-queens and laying-sisters ;
and the ever-dwindling band of the old stock
worked themselves bald and fray-winged to feed
their queer charges. Most of the Oddities would
not, and many, on account of their malformations,
could not, go through a day's field-work ; but
the Wax-moths, who were always busy on the
brood-comb, found pleasant home occupations for
them. One albino, for instance, divided the
number of pounds of honey in stock by the number of bees in the Hive, and proved that if every
bee only gathered honey for seven and three-
quarter minutes a day, she would have the rest of
the time to herself, and could accompany the

drones on their mating flights. The drones were
not at all pleased.

Another, an eyeless drone with no feelers,
said that all brood-cells should be perfect circles,
so as not to interfere with the grub or the workers.
He proved that the old six-sided cell was solely
due to the workers building against each other on
opposite sides of the wall, and that if there were
no interference, there would be no angles. Some
bees tried the new plan for a while, and found it
cost eight times more wax than the old six-sided
specification; and, as they never allowed a
cluster to hang up and make wax in peace, real
wax was scarce. However, they eked out their
task with varnish stolen from new coffins at
funerals, and it made them rather sick. Then
they took to cadging round sugar-factories and
breweries, because it was easiest to get their
material from those places. But the mixture of
glucose and beer naturally fermented in store and
blew the store-cells out of shape, besides smelling
abominably. Some of the sound bees warned
them that ill-gotten gains never prosper, but the
Oddities at once surrounded them and balled them
to death. That was a punishment they were
almost as fond of as they were of eating, and they
expected the sound bees to feed them. Curiously enough, the age-old instinct of loyalty and
devotion towards the Hive made the sound bees do
this, though their reason told them they ought to
slip away and unite with some other healthy stock
in the apiary.

'What about seven and three-quarter minutes'

work now?' said Melissa one day as she came in.
' I've been at it for five hours, and I've only half
a load.'

' Oh, the Hive subsists on the Hival Honey
which the Hive produces,' said a blind Oddity
squatting in a store-cell.

' But honey is gathered from flowers outside—
two miles away sometimes,' cried Melissa.

' Pardon me,' said the blind thing, sucking
hard. ' But this is the Hive, is it not?'

' It was. Worse luck, it is.'

' And the Hival Honey is here, is it not?' It
opened a fresh store-cell to prove it.

' Ye—es, but it won't be long at this rate,'
said Melissa.

' The rates have nothing to do with it. This
Hive produces the Hival Honey. You people
never seem to grasp the economic simplicity that
underlies all life.'

' Oh, me!' said poor Melissa. ' Haven't you
ever been beyond the Gate?'

' Certainly not. A fool's eyes are in the ends
of the earth. Mine are in my head.' It gorged
till it bloated.

Melissa took refuge in her poorly paid field-
work and told Sacharissa the story.

' Hut!' said that wise bee, fretting with an old
maid of a thistle. ' Tell us something new. The
Hive's full of such as him—it, I mean.'

' What's the end to be? All the honey going
out and none coming in. Things *can't* last this
way!' said Melissa.

' Who cares?' said Sacharissa. ' I know now

how drones feel the day before they're killed.   A
short life and a merry one for me ! '

' If it only were merry ! But think of those
awful, solemn, lop-sided Oddities waiting for us
at home—crawling and clambering and preaching
—and dirtying things in the dark.'

' I don't mind that so much as their silly songs,
after we've fed 'em, all about " work among the
merry, merry blossoms," ' said Sacharissa from
the deeps of a stale Canterbury bell.

' I do.   How's our Queen ? ' said Melissa.

' Cheerfully hopeless, as usual. But she lays
an egg now and then.'

' Does she so ? ' Melissa backed out of the
next bell with a jerk. ' Suppose, now, we sound
workers tried to raise a Princess in some clean
corner ? '

' You'd be put to it to find one. The Hive's
all wax-moth and muckings. But—— Well ? '

' A Princess might help us in the time of the
Voice behind the Veil that the Queen talks of.
And anything is better than working for Oddities
that chirrup about work that they can't do, and
waste what we bring home.'

' Who cares ? ' said Sacharissa. ' I'm with
you, for the fun of it. The Oddities would ball
us to death, if they knew. Come home, and we'll
begin.'

    .   .   .   .   .

There is no room to tell how the experienced
Melissa found a far-off frame so messed and mis-
handled by abandoned cell-building experiments
that, for very shame, the bees never went there.

How in that ruin she blocked out a Royal Cell of sound wax, but disguised by rubbish till it looked like a kopje among deserted kopjes. How she prevailed upon the hopeless Queen to make one last effort and lay a worthy egg. How the Queen obeyed and died. How her spent carcass was flung out on the rubbish-heap, and how a multitude of laying-sisters went about dropping drone-eggs where they listed, and said there was no more need of Queens. How, covered by this confusion, Sacharissa educated certain young bees to educate certain new-born bees in the almost lost art of making Royal Jelly. How the nectar for it was won out of hours in the teeth of chill winds. How the hidden egg hatched true—no drone, but Blood Royal. How it was capped, and how desperately they worked to feed and double-feed the now swarming Oddities, lest any break in the food-supplies should set them to instituting inquiries, which, with songs about work, was their favourite amusement. How in an auspicious hour, on a moonless night, the Princess came forth—a Princess indeed,—and how Melissa smuggled her into a dark empty honey-magazine, to bide her time; and how the drones, knowing she was there, went about singing the deep disreputable love-songs of the old days—to the scandal of the laying-sisters, who do not think well of drones. These things are written in the Book of Queens, which is laid up in the hollow of the Great Ash Ygdrasil.

After a few days the weather changed again and became glorious. Even the Oddities would now join the crowd that hung out on the alighting-board, and would sing of work among the merry, merry blossoms till an untrained ear might have received it for the hum of a working hive. Yet, in truth, their store-honey had been eaten long ago. They lived from day to day on the efforts of the few sound bees, while the Wax-moth fretted and consumed again their already ruined wax. But the sound bees never mentioned these matters. They knew, if they did, the Oddities would hold a meeting and ball them to death.

'Now you see what we have done,' said the Wax-moths. 'We have created New Material, a New Convention, a New Type, as we said we would.'

'And new possibilities for us,' said the laying-sisters gratefully. 'You have given us a new life's work, vital and paramount.'

'More than that,' chanted the Oddities in the sunshine; 'you have created a new heaven and a new earth. Heaven, cloudless and accessible' (it was a perfect August evening), 'and Earth teeming with the merry, merry blossoms, waiting only our honest toil to turn them all to good. The—er—Aster, and the Crocus, and the—er—Ladies' Smock in her season, the Chrysanthemum after her kind, and the Guelder Rose bringing forth abundantly withal.'

'Oh, Holy Hymettus!' said Melissa, awe-struck. 'I knew they didn't know how honey was made, but they've forgotten the Order of the Flowers! What will become of them?'

A Shadow fell across the alighting-board as the

Bee Master and his son came by. The Oddities crawled in, and a Voice behind a Veil said: ' I've neglected the old Hive too long. Give me the smoker.'

Melissa heard and darted through the Gate. ' Come, oh, come! ' she cried. ' It is the destruction the Old Queen foretold. Princess, come! '

' Really, you are too archaic for words,' said an Oddity in an alley-way. ' A cloud, I admit, may have crossed the sun ; but why hysterics? Above all, why Princesses so late in the day? Are you aware it's the Hival Tea-Time? Let's sing grace.'

Melissa clawed past him with all six legs. Sacharissa had run to what was left of the fertile brood-comb. ' Down and out! ' she called across the brown breadth of it. ' Nurses, guards, fanners, sweepers—out! Never mind the babies. They're better dead. Out, before the Light and the Hot Smoke! '

The Princess's first clear fearless call (Melissa had found her) rose and drummed through all the frames. ' *La Reine le veult! Swarm! Swar-rm! Swar-r-rm!* '

The Hive shook beneath the shattering thunder of a stuck-down quilt being torn back.

' Don't be alarmed, dears,' said the Waxmoths. ' That's our work. Look up, and you'll see the dawn of the New Day.'

Light broke in the top of the Hive as the Queen had prophesied—naked light on the boiling, bewildered bees.

Sacharissa rounded up her rearguard, which dropped headlong off the frame, and joined the Princess's detachment thrusting toward the Gate. Now panic was in full blast, and each sound bee found herself embraced by at least three Oddities. The first instinct of a frightened bee is to break into the stores and gorge herself with honey; but there were no stores left, so the Oddities fought the sound bees.

'You must feed us, or we shall die!' they cried, holding and clutching and slipping, while the silent scared earwigs and little spiders twisted between their legs. 'Think of the Hive, traitors! The Holy Hive!'

'You should have thought before!' cried the sound bees. 'Stay and see the dawn of your New Day.'

They reached the Gate at last over the soft bodies of many to whom they had ministered.

'On! Out! Up!' roared Melissa in the Princess's ear. 'For the Hive's sake! To the Old Oak!'

The Princess left the alighting-board, circled once, flung herself at the lowest branch of the Old Oak, and her little loyal swarm—you could have covered it with a pint mug—followed, hooked, and hung.

'Hold close!' Melissa gasped. 'The old legends have come true! Look!'

The Hive was half hidden by smoke, and Figures moved through the smoke. They heard a frame crack stickily, saw it heaved high and twirled round between enormous hands—a blotched, bulged, and perished horror of grey wax, corrupt brood, and small drone-cells, all covered with crawling Oddities, strange to the sun.

'Why, this isn't a hive! This is a museum of curiosities,' said the Voice behind the Veil. It was only the Bee Master talking to his son.

'Can you blame 'em, father?' said a second voice. 'It's rotten with Wax-moth. See here!'

Another frame came up. A finger poked through it, and it broke away in rustling flakes of ashy rottenness.

'Number Four Frame! That was your mother's pet comb once,' whispered Melissa to the Princess. 'Many's the good egg I've watched her lay there.'

'Aren't you confusing *post hoc* with *propter hoc*?' said the Bee Master. 'Wax-moth only succeed when weak bees let them in.' A third frame crackled and rose into the light. 'All this is full of laying workers' brood. That never happens till the stock's weakened. Phew!'

He beat it on his knee like a tambourine, and it also crumbled to pieces.

The little swarm shivered as they watched the dwarf drone-grubs squirm feebly on the grass. Many sound bees had nursed on that frame, well knowing their work was useless; but the actual sight of even useless work destroys disheartens a good worker.

'No, they have some recuperative power left,' said the second voice. 'Here's a Queen cell!'

'But it's tucked away among—— What on earth *has* come to the little wretches? They seem to have lost the instinct of cell-building.' The father held up the frame where the bees had experimented in circular cell-work. It looked like the pitted head of a decaying toadstool.

'Not altogether,' the son corrected. 'There's one line, at least, of perfectly good cells.'

'My work,' said Sacharissa to herself. 'I'm glad Man does me justice before——'

That frame, too, was smashed out and thrown atop of the others and the foul earwiggy quilts.

As frame after frame followed it, the swarm beheld the upheaval, exposure, and destruction of all that had been well or ill done in every cranny of their Hive for generations past. There was black comb so old that they had forgotten where it hung; orange, buff, and ochre-varnished store-comb, built as bees were used to build before the days of artificial foundations; and there was a little, white, frail new work. There were sheets on sheets of level, even brood-comb that had held in its time unnumbered thousands of unnamed workers; patches of obsolete drone-comb, broad and high-shouldered, showing to what marks the male grub was expected to grow; and two-inch-deep honey-magazines, empty, but still magnificent: the whole gummed and glued into twisted scrapwork, awry on the wires, half-cells, beginnings abandoned, or grandiose, weak-walled, composite cells pieced out with rubbish and capped with dirt.

Good or bad, every inch of it was so riddled

by the tunnels of the Wax-moth that it broke in clouds of dust as it was flung on the heap.

'Oh, see!' cried Sacharissa. 'The Great Burning that Our Queen foretold. Who can bear to look?'

A flame crawled up the pile of rubbish, and they smelt singeing wax.

The Figures stooped, lifted the Hive and shook it upside down over the pyre. A cascade of Oddities, chips of broken comb, scale, fluff, and grubs slid out, crackled, sizzled, popped a little, and then the flames roared up and consumed all that fuel.

'We must disinfect,' said a Voice. 'Get me a sulphur-candle, please.'

The shell of the Hive was returned to its place, a light was set in its sticky emptiness, tier by tier the Figures built it up, closed the entrance, and went away. The swarm watched the light leaking through the cracks all the long night. At dawn one Wax-moth came by, fluttering impudently.

'There has been a miscalculation about the New Day, my dears,' she began; 'one can't expect people to be perfect all at once. That was our mistake.'

'No, the mistake was entirely ours,' said the Princess.

'Pardon me,' said the Wax-moth. 'When you think of the enormous upheaval—call it good or bad—which our influence brought about, you will admit that we, and we alone——'

'You?' said the Princess. 'Our stock was

H

not strong.   So *you* came—as any other disease might have come.   Hang close, all my people.'

When the sun rose, Veiled Figures came down, and saw their swarm at the bough's end waiting patiently within sight of the old Hive—a handful, but prepared to go on.

THE BEES AND THE FLIES

A FARMER of the Augustan age
Perused, in Virgil's golden page,
The story of the secret won
From Proteus by Cyrene's son—
How the dank sea-god showed the swain
Means to restore his hives again :
More briefly, how a slaughtered bull
Breeds honey by the bellyful.

The egregious rustic put to death
A bull by stopping of its breath :
Disposed the carcass in a shed
With fragrant herbs and branches spread ;
And, having thus performed the charm,
Sat down to wait the promised swarm.

Nor waited long.   The God of Day
Impartial, quickening with his ray
Evil and good alike, beheld
The carcass—and the carcass swelled !
Big with new birth the belly heaves
Beneath its screen of scented leaves ;
Past any doubt, the bull conceives !

The farmer bids men bring more hives
To house the profit that arrives ;
Prepares on pan, and key and kettle,
Sweet music that shall make 'em settle ;
But when to crown the work he goes,
Gods ! what a stink salutes his nose !
Where are the honest toilers ?   Where
The gravid mistress of their care ?
A busy scene, indeed, he sees,
But not a sign or sound of bees.
Worms of the riper grave unhid
By any kindly coffin-lid,
Obscene and shameless to the light,
Seethe in insatiate appetite
Through putrid offal ; while above
The hissing blow-fly seeks his love,
Whose offspring, supping where they supt,
Consume corruption twice corrupt.

With the Night Mail

With the Night Mail

(A.D. 1908)

A Story of a.d. 2000

(Together with extracts from the magazine in which it appeared)

At nine o'clock of a gusty winter night I stood
on the lower stages of one of the G.P.O. outward
mail towers. My purpose was a run to Quebec
in ' Postal Packet 162 or such other as may be
appointed ': and the Postmaster-General himself countersigned the order. This talisman
opened all doors, even those in the despatching-
caisson at the foot of the tower, where they were
delivering the sorted Continental mail. The bags
lay packed close as herrings in the long grey
underbodies which our G.P.O. still calls ' coaches.'
Five such coaches were filled as I watched, and
were shot up the guides to be locked on to
their waiting packets three hundred feet nearer
the stars.

From the despatching-caisson I was conducted
by a courteous and wonderfully learned official—
Mr. L. L. Geary, Second Despatcher of the
Western Route—to the Captains' Room (this

wakes an echo of old romance), where the Mail captains come on for their turn of duty. He introduces me to the Captain of ' 162 '—Captain Purnall, and his relief, Captain Hodgson. The one is small and dark; the other large and red; but each has the brooding sheathed glance characteristic of eagles and aeronauts. You can see it in the pictures of our racing professionals, from L. V. Rautsch to little Ada Warrleigh—that fathomless abstraction of eyes habitually turned through naked space.

On the notice-board in the Captains' Room, the pulsing arrows of some twenty indicators register, degree by geographical degree, the progress of as many homeward-bound packets. The word ' Cape ' rises across the face of a dial; a gong strikes: the South African mid-weekly mail is in at the Highgate Receiving Towers. That is all. It reminds one comically of the traitorous little bell which in pigeon-fanciers' lofts notifies the return of a homer.

' Time for us to be on the move,' says Captain Purnall, and we are shot up by the passenger-lift to the top of the despatch-towers. ' Our coach will lock on when it is filled and the clerks are aboard.' . . .

'No. 162' waits for us in Slip E of the topmost stage. The great curve of her back shines frostily under the lights, and some minute alteration of trim makes her rock a little in her holding-down slips.

Captain Purnall frowns and dives inside. Hissing softly, ' 162 ' comes to rest as level as a rule.

From her North Atlantic Winter nose-cap (worn bright as diamond with boring through uncounted leagues of hail, snow, and ice) to the inset of her three built-out propeller-shafts is some two hundred and forty feet. Her extreme diameter, carried well forward, is thirty-seven. Contrast this with the nine hundred by ninety-five of any crack liner, and you will realise the power that must drive a hull through all weathers at more than the emergency speed of the *Cyclonic*!

The eye detects no joint in her skin plating save the sweeping hair-crack of the bow-rudder— Magniac's rudder which assured us the dominion of the unstable air and left its inventor penniless and half-blind. It is calculated to Castelli's ' gull-wing ' curve. Raise a few feet of that all but invisible plate three-eighths of an inch and she will yaw five miles to port or starboard ere she is under control again. Give her full helm and she returns on her track like a whip-lash. Cant the whole forward—a touch on the wheel will suffice— and she sweeps at your good direction up or down. Open the complete circle and she presents to the air a mushroom-head that will bring her up all standing within a half mile.

' Yes,' says Captain Hodgson, answering my thought, ' Castelli thought he'd discovered the secret of controlling aeroplanes when he'd only found out how to steer dirigible balloons. Magniac invented his rudder to help war-boats ram each other; and war went out of fashion and Magniac he went out of his mind because he said he couldn't serve his country any more. I wonder if any of us ever know what we're really doing.'

'If you want to see the coach locked you'd better go aboard. It's due now,' says Mr. Geary. I enter through the door amidships. There is nothing here for display. The inner skin of the gas-tank comes down to within a foot or two of my head and turns over just short of the turn of the bilges. Liners and yachts disguise their tanks with decoration, but the G.P.O. serves them raw under a lick of grey official paint. The inner skin shuts off fifty feet of the bow and as much of the stern, but the bow-bulkhead is recessed for the lift-shunting apparatus as the stern is pierced for the shaft-tunnels. The engine-room lies almost amidships. Forward of it, extending to the turn of the bow tanks, is an aperture—a bottomless hatch at present—into which our coach will be locked. One looks down over the coamings three hundred feet to the despatching-caisson whence voices boom upward. The light below is obscured to a sound of thunder, as our coach rises on its guides. It enlarges rapidly from a postage-stamp to a playing-card; to a punt and last a pontoon. The two clerks, its crew, do not even look up as it comes into place. The Quebec letters fly under their fingers and leap into the docketed racks, while both captains and Mr. Geary satisfy themselves that the coach is locked home. A clerk passes the way-bill over the hatch-coaming. Captain Purnall thumb-marks and passes it to Mr. Geary. Receipt has been given and taken. 'Pleasant run,' says Mr. Geary, and disappears through the door which a foot-high pneumatic compressor locks after him.

' A-ah ! ' sighs the compressor released. Our holding-down clips part with a tang. We are clear.

Captain Hodgson opens the great colloid under-body-porthole through which I watch overlighted London slide eastward as the gale gets hold of us. The first of the low winter clouds cuts off the well-known view and darkens Middlesex. On the south edge of it I can see a postal packet's light ploughing through the white fleece. For an instant she gleams like a star ere she drops toward the Highgate Receiving Towers. ' The Bombay Mail,' says Captain Hodgson, and looks at his watch. ' She's forty minutes late.'

' What's our level ? ' I ask.

' Four thousand. Aren't you coming up on the bridge ? '

The bridge (let us ever praise the G.P.O. as a repository of ancientest tradition !) is repre-sented by a view of Captain Hodgson's legs where he stands on the Control Platform that runs thwartships overhead. The bow colloid is un-shuttered and Captain Purnall, one hand on the wheel, is feeling for a fair slant. The dial shows 4300 feet.

' It's steep to-night,' he mutters, as tier on tier of cloud drops under. ' We generally pick up an easterly draught below three thousand at this time o' the year. I hate slathering through fluff.'

' So does Van Cutsem. Look at him huntin'

for a slant!' says Captain Hodgson. A fog-light breaks cloud a hundred fathoms below. The Antwerp Night Mail makes her signal and rises between two racing clouds far to port, her flanks blood-red in the glare of Sheerness Double Light. The gale will have us over the North Sea in half an hour, but Captain Purnall lets her go composedly—nosing to every point of the compass as she rises.

'Five thousand—six, six thousand eight hundred'—the dip-dial reads ere we find the easterly drift, heralded by a flurry of snow at the thousand fathom level. Captain Purnall rings up the engines and keys down the governor on the switch before him. There is no sense in urging machinery when Aeolus himself gives you good knots for nothing. We are away in earnest now —our nose notched home on our chosen star. At this level the lower clouds are laid out, all neatly combed by the dry fingers of the East. Below that again is the strong westerly blow through which we rose. Overhead, a film of southerly drifting mist draws a theatrical gauze across the firmament. The moonlight turns the lower strata to silver without a stain except where our shadow underruns us. Bristol and Cardiff Double Lights (those statelily inclined beams over Severnmouth) are dead ahead of us; for we keep the Southern Winter Route. Coventry Central, the pivot of the English system, stabs upward once in ten seconds its spear of diamond light to the north; and a point or two off our starboard bow The Leek, the great cloud-breaker of Saint

David's Head, swings its unmistakable green beam twenty-five degrees each way. There must be half a mile of fluff over it in this weather, but it does not affect The Leek.

'Our planet's overlighted if anything,' says Captain Purnall at the wheel, as Cardiff-Bristol slides under. 'I remember the old days of common white verticals that 'ud show two or three hundred feet up in a mist, if you knew where to look for 'em. In really fluffy weather they might as well have been under your hat. One could get lost coming home then, an' have some fun. Now it's like driving down Piccadilly.'

He points to the pillars of light where the cloud-breakers bore through the cloud-floor. We see nothing of England's outlines: only a white pavement pierced in all directions by these man-holes of variously coloured fire—Holy Island's white and red—St. Bees' interrupted white, and so on as far as the eye can reach. Blessed be Sargent, Ahrens, and the Dubois brothers, who invented the cloud-breakers of the world whereby we travel in security!

'Are you going to lift for The Shamrock?' asks Captain Hodgson. Cork Light (green, fixed) enlarges as we rush to it. Captain Purnall nods. There is heavy traffic hereabouts—the cloud-bank beneath us is streaked with running fissures of flame where the Atlantic boats are hurrying Londonward just clear of the fluff. Mail-packets are supposed, under the Conference rules, to have the five-thousand-foot lanes to themselves, but the foreigner in a hurry is apt to take liberties with

English air. 'No. 162' lifts to a long-drawn wail of the breeze in the fore-flange of the rudder and we make Valencia (white, green, white) at a safe 7000 feet, dipping our beam to an incoming Washington packet.

There is no cloud on the Atlantic, and faint streaks of cream round Dingle Bay show where the driven seas hammer the coast. A big S.A.T.A. liner (*Société Anonyme des Transports Aériens*) is diving and lifting half a mile below us in search of some break in the solid west wind. Lower still lies a disabled Dane: she is telling the liner all about it in International. Our General Communication dial has caught her talk and begins to eavesdrop. Captain Hodgson makes a motion to shut it off but checks himself. 'Perhaps you'd like to listen,' he says.

'*Argol* of St. Thomas,' the Dane whimpers. 'Report owners three starboard shaft collar-bearings fused. Can make Flores as we are, but impossible farther. Shall we buy spares at Fayal?'

The liner acknowledges and recommends inverting the bearings. The *Argol* answers that she has already done so without effect, and begins to relieve her mind about cheap German enamels for collar-bearings. The Frenchman assents cordially, cries '*Courage, mon ami,*' and switches off.

Their lights sink under the curve of the ocean.

'That's one of Lundt & Bleamers's boats,' says Captain Hodgson. 'Serves 'em right for putting German compos in their thrust-blocks.

She won't be in Fayal to-night! By the way, wouldn't you like to look round the engine-room?'

I have been waiting eagerly for this invitation and I follow Captain Hodgson from the control-platform, stooping low to avoid the bulge of the tanks. We know that Fleury's gas can lift any-thing, as the world-famous trials of '89 showed, but its almost indefinite powers of expansion necessitate vast tank-room. Even in this thin air the lift-shunts are busy taking out one-third of its normal lift, and still '162' must be checked by an occasional down-draw of the rudder or our flight would become a climb to the stars. Captain Purnall prefers an overlifted to an underlifted ship; but no two captains trim ship alike. 'When *I* take the bridge,' says Captain Hodgson, 'you'll see me shunt forty per cent of the lift out of the gas and run her on the upper rudder. With a swoop upwards instead of a swoop downwards, *as* you say. Either way will do. It's only habit. Watch our dip-dial! Tim fetches her down once every thirty knots as regularly as breathing.'

So is it shown on the dip-dial. For five or six minutes the arrow creeps from 6700 to 7300. There is the faint 'szgee' of the rudder, and back slides the arrow to 6000 on a falling slant of ten or fifteen knots.

'In heavy weather you jockey her with the screws as well,' says Captain Hodgson, and, un-clipping the jointed bar which divides the engine-room from the bare deck, he leads me on to the floor.

Here we find Fleury's Paradox of the Bulk-headed Vacuum—which we accept now without thought—literally in full blast. The three engines are H. T. & T. assisted-vacuo Fleury turbines running from 3000 to the Limit—that is to say, up to the point when the blades make the air 'bell'—cut out a vacuum for themselves precisely as over-driven marine propellers used to do. '162's' Limit is low on account of the small size of her nine screws, which, though handier than the old colloid Thelussons, 'bell' sooner. The midships engine, generally used as a reinforce, is not running; so the port and starboard turbine vacuum-chambers draw direct into the return-mains.

The turbines whistle reflectively. From the low-arched expansion-tanks on either side the valves descend pillarwise to the turbine-chests, and thence the obedient gas whirls through the spirals of blades with a force that would whip the teeth out of a power-saw. Behind, is its own pressure held in leash or spurred on by the lift-shunts; before it, the vacuum where Fleury's Ray dances in violet-green bands and whirled tourbillons of flame. The jointed U-tubes of the vacuum-chamber are pressure-tempered colloid (no glass would endure the strain for an instant) and a junior engineer with tinted spectacles watches the Ray intently. It is the very heart of the machine—a mystery to this day. Even Fleury who begat it and, unlike Magniac, died a multi-millionaire, could not explain how the restless little imp shuddering in the U-tube can, in the

fractional fraction of a second, strike the furious
blast of gas into a chill greyish-green liquid that
drains (you can hear it trickle) from the far end
of the vacuum through the eduction-pipes and
the mains back to the bilges. Here it returns to
its gaseous, one had almost written sagacious,
state and climbs to work afresh. Bilge-tank, upper
tank, dorsal-tank, expansion-chamber, vacuum,
main-return (as a liquid), and bilge-tank once
more is the ordained cycle. Fleury's Ray sees to
that; and the engineer with the tinted spectacles
sees to Fleury's Ray. If a speck of oil, if even
the natural grease of the human finger, touch the
hooded terminals Fleury's Ray will wink and dis-
appear and must be laboriously built up again.
This means half a day's work for all hands and an
expense of one hundred and seventy-odd pounds
to the G.P.O. for radium-salts and such trifles.

' Now look at our thrust-collars. You won't
find much German compo there. Full-jewelled,
you see,' says Captain Hodgson as the engineer
shunts open the top of a cap. Our shaft-bearings
are C.M.C. (Commercial Minerals Company)
stones, ground with as much care as the lens of a
telescope. They cost £37 apiece. So far we have
not arrived at their term of life. These bearings
came from ' No. 97,' which took them over from
the old *Dominion of Light*, which had them out
of the wreck of the *Perseus* aeroplane in the years
when men still flew tin kites over oil engines!

They are a shining reproof to all low-grade
German ' ruby ' enamels, so-called ' boort ' facings,
and the dangerous and unsatisfactory alumina

I

compounds which please dividend-hunting owners and drive skippers crazy.

The rudder-gear and the gas lift-shunt, seated side by side under the engine-room dials, are the only machines in visible motion. The former sighs from time to time as the oil plunger rises and falls half an inch. The latter, cased and guarded like the U-tube aft, exhibits another Fleury Ray, but inverted and more green than violet. Its function is to shunt the lift out of the gas, and this it will do without watching. That is all! A tiny pump-rod wheezing and whining to itself beside a sputtering green lamp. A hundred and fifty feet aft down the flat-topped tunnel of the tanks a violet light, restless and irresolute. Between the two, three white-painted turbine-trunks, like eel-baskets laid on their side, accentuate the empty perspectives. You can hear the trickle of the liquefied gas flowing from the vacuum into the bilge-tanks and the soft *gluck-glock* of gas-locks closing as Captain Purnall brings ' 162 ' down by the head. The hum of the turbines and the boom of the air on our skin is no more than a cotton-wool wrapping to the universal stillness. And we are running an eighteen-second mile.

I peer from the fore end of the engine-room over the hatch-coamings into the coach. The mail-clerks are sorting the Winnipeg, Calgary, and Medicine Hat bags; but there is a pack of cards ready on the table.

Suddenly a bell thrills; the engineers run to the turbine-valves and stand by; but the spectacled

Slave of the Ray in the U-tube never lifts his head. He must watch where he is. We are hard-braked and going astern; there is language from the Control Platform.

'Tim's sparking badly about something,' says the unruffled Captain Hodgson. 'Let's look.'

Captain Purnall is not the suave man we left half an hour since, but the embodied authority of the G.P.O.   Ahead of us floats an ancient, aluminium-patched, twin-screw tramp of the dingiest, with no more right to the 5000-foot lane than has a horse-cart to a modern road.   She carries an obsolete 'barbette' conning-tower—a six-foot affair with railed platform forward—and our warning beam plays on the top of it as a police-man's lantern flashes on the area sneak.   Like a sneak-thief, too, emerges a shock-headed navigator in his shirt-sleeves.   Captain Purnall wrenches open the colloid to talk with him man to man. There are times when Science does not satisfy.

'What under the stars are you doing here, you sky-scraping chimney-sweep?' he shouts as we two drift side by side. 'Do you know this is a Mail-lane? You call yourself a sailor, sir? You ain't fit to peddle toy balloons to an Esquimaux. Your name and number! Report and get down, and be—— !'

'I've been blown up once,' the shock-headed man cries, hoarsely as a dog barking. 'I don't care two flips of a contact for anything *you* can do, Postey.'

'Don't you, sir? But I'll make you care. I'll have you towed stern first to Disko and broke up. You can't recover insurance if you're broke for obstruction. Do you understand *that*?'

Then the stranger bellows: 'Look at my propellers! There's been a wulli-wa down below that has knocked us into umbrella-frames! We've been blown up about forty thousand feet! We're all one conjuror's watch inside! My mate's arm's broke; my engineer's head's cut open; my Ray went out when the engines smashed; and ... and ... for pity's sake give me my height, Captain! We doubt we're dropping.'

'Six thousand eight hundred. Can you hold it?' Captain Purnall overlooks all insults, and leans half out of the colloid, staring and sniffing. The stranger leaks pungently.

'We ought to blow into St. John's with luck. We're trying to plug the fore-tank now, but she's simply whistling it away,' her captain wails.

'She's sinking like a log,' says Captain Purnall in an undertone. 'Call up the Banks Mark Boat, George.' Our dip-dial shows that we, keeping abreast the tramp, have dropped five hundred feet the last few minutes.

Captain Purnall presses a switch and our signal beam begins to swing through the night, twizzling spokes of light across infinity.

'That'll fetch something,' he says, while Captain Hodgson watches the General Communicator. He has called up the North Banks Mark Boat, a few hundred miles west, and is reporting the case.

'I'll stand by you,' Captain Purnall roars to the lone figure on the conning-tower.

'Is it as bad as that?' comes the answer. 'She isn't insured. She's mine.'

'Might have guessed as much,' mutters Hodgson. 'Owner's risk is the worst risk of all!'

'Can't I fetch St. John's—not even with this breeze?' the voice quavers.

'Stand by to abandon ship. Haven't you *any* lift in you, fore or aft?'

'Nothing but the midship tanks, and they're none too tight. You see, my Ray gave out and ——' He coughs in the reek of the escaping gas.

'You poor devil!' This does not reach our friend. 'What does the Mark Boat say, George?'

'Wants to know if there's any danger to traffic. Says she's in a bit of weather herself and can't quit station. I've turned in a General Call, so even if they don't see our beam some one's bound to help—or else *we* must. Shall I clear our slings? Hold on! Here we are! A Planet liner, too! She'll be up in a tick!'

'Tell her to have her slings ready,' cries his brother captain. 'There won't be much time to spare. . . . Tie up your mate,' he roars to the tramp.

'My mate's all right. It's my engineer. He's gone crazy.'

'Shunt the lift out of him with a spanner. Hurry!'

'But I can make St. John's if you'll stand by.'

'You'll make the deep, wet Atlantic in twenty

minutes.   You're less than fifty-eight hundred now.   Get your papers.'

A Planet liner, east bound, heaves up in a superb spiral and takes the air of us humming. Her underbody colloid is open and her transporter-slings hang down like tentacles.   We shut off our beam as she adjusts herself—steering to a hair—over the tramp's conning-tower.   The mate comes up, his arm strapped to his side, and stumbles into the cradle.   A man with a ghastly scarlet head follows, shouting that he must go back and build up his Ray.   The mate assures him that he will find a nice new Ray all ready in the liner's engine-room.   The bandaged head goes up wagging excitedly.   A youth and a woman follow.   The liner cheers hollowly above us, and we see the passengers' faces at the saloon colloid.

' That's a pretty girl.   What's the fool waiting for now?' says Captain Purnall.

The skipper comes up, still appealing to us to stand by and see him fetch St. John's.   He dives below and returns—at which we little human beings in the void cheer louder than ever—with the ship's kitten.   Up fly the liner's hissing slings;   her underbody crashes home and she hurtles away again.   The dial shows less than 3000 feet.

The Mark Boat signals we must attend to the derelict, now whistling her death-song, as she falls beneath us in long sick zigzags.

' Keep our beam on her and send out a General Warning,' says Captain Purnall, following her down.

There is no need. Not a liner in air but knows the meaning of that vertical beam and gives us and our quarry a wide berth.

' But she'll drown in the water, won't she? ' I ask.

' Not always,' is his answer. ' I've known a derelict up-end and sift her engines out of herself and flicker round the Lower Lanes for three weeks on her forward tanks only. We'll run no risks. Pith her, George, and look sharp. There's weather ahead.'

Captain Hodgson opens the underbody colloid, swings the heavy pithing-iron out of its rack, which in liners is generally cased as a smoking-room settee, and at two hundred feet releases the catch. We hear the whir of the crescent-shaped arms opening as they descend. The derelict's forehead is punched in, starred across, and rent diagonally. She falls stern first, our beam upon her; slides like a lost soul down that pitiless ladder of light, and the Atlantic takes her.

' A filthy business,' says Hodgson. ' I wonder what it must have been like in the old days? '

The thought had crossed my mind too. What if that wavering carcass had been filled with the men of the old days, each one of them taught (*that* is the horror of it !) that after death he would very possibly go for ever to unspeakable torment?

And scarcely a generation ago, we (one knows now that we are only our fathers re-enlarged upon the earth), *we*, I say, ripped and rammed and pithed to admiration.

Here Tim, from the Control Platform, shouts

that we are to get into our inflators and to bring him his at once.

We hurry into the heavy rubber suits—the engineers are already dressed—and inflate at the air-pump taps. G.P.O. inflators are thrice as thick as a racing man's ' flickers,' and chafe abominably under the armpits. George takes the wheel until Tim has blown himself up to the extreme of rotundity. If you kicked him off the c.p. to the deck he would bounce back. But it is ' 162 ' that will do the kicking.

' The Mark Boat's mad—stark ravin' crazy,' he snorts, returning to command. ' She says there's a bad blow-out ahead and wants me to pull over to Greenland. I'll see her pithed first ! We wasted half an hour fussing over that dead duck down under, and now I'm expected to go rubbin' my back all round the Pole. What does she think a postal packet's made of? Gummed silk? Tell her we're coming on straight, George.'

George buckles him into the Frame and switches on the Direct Control. Now under Tim's left toe lies the port-engine Accelerator ; under his left heel the Reverse, and so with the other foot. The lift-shunt stops stand out on the rim of the steering-wheel where the fingers of his left hand can play on them. At his right hand is the midships engine-lever ready to be thrown into gear at a moment's notice. He leans forward in his belt, eyes glued to the colloid, and one ear cocked toward the General Communicator. Henceforth he is the strength and direction of ' 162,' through whatever may befall.

The Banks Mark Boat is reeling out pages of
A.B.C. Directions to the traffic at large. We are
to secure all ' loose objects ' ; hood up our Fleury
Rays ; and ' on no account to attempt to clear
snow from our conning-towers till the weather
abates.'   Under-powered craft, we are told, can
ascend to the limit of their lift, mail-packets to
look out for them accordingly.   The lower lanes
westward are pitting very badly, ' with frequent
blow-outs, vortices, laterals, etc.'

Still the clear dark holds up unblemished.   The
only warning is the electric skin-tension (I feel as
though I were a lace-maker's pillow) and an irri-
tability which the gibbering of the General
Communicator increases almost to hysteria.

We have made eight thousand feet since we
pithed the tramp and our turbines are giving us
an honest two hundred and ten knots.

Very far to the west an elongated blur of red,
low down, shows us the North Banks Mark Boat.
There are specks of fire round her rising and
falling—bewildered planets about an unstable
sun—helpless shipping hanging on to her light
for company's sake.   No wonder she could not
quit station.

She warns us to look out for the back-wash of
the bad vortex in which (her beam shows it) she is
even now reeling.

The pits of gloom about us begin to fill with
very faintly luminous films—wreathing and uneasy shapes.   One forms itself into a globe of pale
flame that waits shivering with eagerness till we
sweep by.   It leaps monstrously across the black-

ness, alights on the precise top of our nose, pirouettes there an instant, and swings off. Our roaring bow sinks as though that light were lead —sinks and recovers to lurch and stumble again beneath the next blow-out. Tim's fingers on the lift-shunt strike chords of numbers—1 : 4 : 7 :— 2 : 4 : 6 :—7 : 5 : 3, and so on; for he is running by his tanks only, lifting or lowering her against the uneasy air. All three engines are at work, for the sooner we have skated over this thin ice the better. Higher we dare not go. The whole upper vault is charged with pale krypton vapours, which our skin-friction may excite to unholy manifestations. Between the upper and lower levels—5000 and 7000, hints the Mark Boat— we may perhaps bolt through if . . . Our bow clothes itself in blue flame and falls like a sword. No human skill can keep pace with the changing tensions. A vortex has us by the beak and we dive down a two-thousand-foot slant at an angle (the dip-dial and my bouncing body record it) of thirty-five. Our turbines scream shrilly; the propellers cannot bite on the vexed air; Tim shunts the lift out of five tanks at once and by sheer weight drives her bulletwise through the maelstrom till she cushions with a jar on an up-gust, three thousand feet below.

'*Now* we've done it,' says George in my ear. 'Our skin-friction, that last slide, has played Old Harry with the tensions! Look out for laterals, Tim; she'll want some holding.'

I've got her,' is the answer. 'Come *up*, old woman.'

She comes up nobly, but the laterals buffet her left and right like the pinions of angry angels. She is jolted off her course four ways at once, and cuffed into place again, only to be swung aside and dropped into a new chaos. We are never without a corposant grinning on our bows or rolling head over heels from nose to midships, and to the crackle of electricity around and within us is added once or twice the rattle of hail—hail that will never fall on any sea. Slow we must, or we may break our back, pitch-poling.

'Air's a perfectly elastic fluid,' roars George above the tumult. 'About as elastic as a head-sea off the Fastnet, ain't it?'

He is less than just to the good element. If one intrudes on the Heavens when they are balancing their volt-accounts; if one disturbs the High Gods' market-rates by hurling steel hulls at ninety knots across tremblingly adjusted electric tensions, one must not complain of any rudeness in the reception. Tim met it with an unmoved countenance, one corner of his under-lip caught up on a tooth, his eyes fleeting into the blackness twenty miles ahead, and the fierce sparks flying from his knuckles at every turn of the hand. Now and again he shook his head to clear the sweat trickling from his eyebrows, and it was then that George, watching his chance, would slide down the life-rail and swab his face quickly with a big red handkerchief. I never imagined that a human being could so continuously labour and so collectedly think as did Tim through that Hell's half-hour when the flurry

was at its worst. We were dragged hither and
yon by warm or frozen suctions, belched up on
the tops of wulli-was, spun down by vortices and
clubbed aside by laterals under a dizzying rush
of stars in the company of a drunken moon.   I
heard the rushing click of the midships engine-
lever sliding in and out, the low growl of the lift-
shunts, and, louder than the yelling winds without,
the scream of the bow-rudder gouging into any
lull that promised hold for an instant. At last we
began to claw up on a cant, bow-rudder and port-
propeller together. Only the nicest balancing of
tanks saved us from spinning like the rifle-bullet
of the old days.

'We've got to hitch to windward of that Mark
Boat somehow,' George cried.

'There's no windward,' I protested feebly,
where I swung shackled to a stanchion. 'How
can there be?'

He laughed—as we pitched into a thousand-
foot blow-out—that red man laughed beneath his
inflated hood!

'Look!' he said. 'We must clear those
refugees with a high lift.'

The Mark Boat was below and a little to the
sou'-west of us, fluctuating in the centre of her
distraught galaxy. The air was thick with moving
lights at every level. I take it most of them were
trying to lie head to wind but, not being hydras,
they failed. An under-tanked Moghrabi boat had
risen to the limit of her lift, and, finding no improvement, had dropped a couple of thousand.
There she met a superb wulli-wa, and was blown

up spinning like a dead leaf. Instead of shutting off she went astern and, naturally, rebounded as from a wall almost into the Mark Boat, whose language (our G.C. took it in) was humanly simple.

'If they'd only ride it out quietly it 'ud be better,' said George in a calm, while we climbed like a bat above them all. 'But some skippers *will* navigate without enough lift. What does that Tad-boat think she is doing, Tim?'

'Playin' kiss in the ring,' was Tim's unmoved reply. A Trans-Asiatic Direct liner had found a smooth and butted into it full power. But there was a vortex at the tail of that smooth, so the T.A.D. was flipped out like a pea from off a finger-nail, braking madly as she fled down and all but over-ending.

'Now I hope she's satisfied,' said Tim. 'I'm glad I'm not a Mark Boat . . . Do I want help?' The General Communicator dial had caught his ear. 'George, you may tell that gentleman with my love,—love, remember, George—that I do not want help. Who *is* the officious sardine-tin?'

'A Rimouski drogher on the look-out for a tow.'

'Very kind of the Rimouski drogher. This postal packet isn't being towed at present.'

'Those droghers will go anywhere on a chance of salvage,' George explained. 'We call 'em kittiwakes.'

A long-beaked, bright steel ninety-footer floated at ease for one instant within hail of us,

her slings coiled ready for rescues, and a single
hand in her open tower. He was smoking. Surrendered to the insurrection of the airs through
which we tore our way, he lay in absolute peace.
I saw the smoke of his pipe ascend untroubled
ere his boat dropped, it seemed, like a stone in a
well.

We had just cleared the Mark Boat and her
disorderly neighbours when the storm ended
as suddenly as it had begun. A shooting-
star to northward filled the sky with the green
blink of a meteorite dissipating itself in our
atmosphere.

Said George: 'That may iron out all the
tensions.' Even as he spoke, the conflicting
winds came to rest; the levels filled; the laterals
died out in long easy swells; the air-ways were
smoothed before us. In less than three minutes
the covey round the Mark Boat had shipped their
power-lights and whirred away upon their busi-
nesses.

'What's happened?' I gasped. The nerve-
storm within and the volt-tingle without had
passed: my inflators weighed like lead.

'God, He knows!' said Captain George
soberly. 'That old shooting-star's skin-friction
has discharged the different levels. I've seen it
happen before. Phew! What a relief!'

We dropped from ten to six thousand and got
rid of our clammy suits. Tim shut off and stepped
out of the Frame. The Mark Boat was coming
up behind us. He opened the colloid in that
heavenly stillness and mopped his face.

'Hello, Williams!' he cried. 'A degree or two out o' station, ain't you?'

'Maybe,' was the answer from the Mark Boat. 'I've had some company this evening.'

'So I noticed. Wasn't that quite a little draught?'

'I warned you. Why didn't you pull out north? The east-bound packets have.'

'Me? Not till I'm running a Polar consumptives' Sanatorium boat. I was squinting through a colloid before you were out of your cradle, my son.'

'I'd be the last man to deny it,' the captain of the Mark Boat replies softly. 'The way you handled her just now—I'm a pretty fair judge of traffic in a volt-flurry—it was a thousand revolutions beyond anything even *I*'ve ever seen.'

Tim's back supples visibly to this oiling. Captain George on the c.p. winks and points to the portrait of a singularly attractive maiden pinned up on Tim's telescope-bracket above the steering-wheel.

I see. Wholly and entirely do I see!

There is some talk overhead of 'coming round to tea on Friday,' a brief report of the derelict's fate, and Tim volunteers as he descends: 'For an A.B.C. man young Williams is less of a high-tension fool than some . . . Were you thinking of taking her on, George? Then I'll just have a look round that port-thrust—seems to me it's a trifle warm—and we'll jog along.'

The Mark Boat hums off joyously and hangs herself up in her appointed eyrie. Here she will

stay, a shutterless observatory ; a life-boat station ;
a salvage tug ; a court of ultimate appeal-cum-
meteorological bureau for three hundred miles
in all directions, till Wednesday next when her
relief slides across the stars to take her buffeted
place.   Her black hull, double conning-tower, and
ever-ready slings represent all that remains to the
planet of that odd old word Authority.   She is
responsible only to the Aerial Board of Control—
the A.B.C. of which Tim speaks so flippantly.
But that semi-elected, semi-nominated body of a
few score persons of both sexes controls this
planet.   'Transportation is Civilisation,' our
motto runs.   Theoretically, we do what we please
so long as we do not interfere with the traffic *and
all it implies*.   Practically, the A.B.C. confirms or
annuls all international arrangements and, to
judge from its last report, finds our tolerant,
humorous, lazy little planet only too ready to
shift the whole burden of public administration
on to its shoulders.

I discuss this with Tim, sipping maté on the
c.p. while George fans her along over the white
blur of the Banks in beautiful upward curves of
fifty miles each.   The dip-dial translates them on
the tape in flowing freehand.

Tim gathers up a skein of it and surveys the
last few feet, which record ' 162's ' path through
the volt-flurry.

' I haven't had a fever-chart like this to show
up in five years,' he says ruefully.

A postal packet's dip-dials record every yard of
every run.   The tapes then go to the A.B.C.,

which collates and makes composite photographs of them for the instruction of Captains. Tim studies his irrevocable past, shaking his head.

'Hello! Here's a fifteen-hundred-foot drop at fifty-five degrees! We must have been standing on our heads then, George.'

'You don't say so,' George answers. 'I fancied I noticed it at the time.'

George may not have Captain Purnall's catlike swiftness, but he is all an artist to the tips of the broad fingers that play on the shunt-stops. The delicious flight-curves come away on the tape with never a waver. The Mark Boat's vertical spindle of light lies down to eastward, setting in the face of the following stars. Westward, where no planet should rise, the triple verticals of Trinity Bay (we keep still to the Southern route) make a low-lifting haze. We seem the only thing at rest under all the heavens; floating at ease till the earth's revolution shall turn up our landing-towers.

And minute by minute our silent clock gives us a sixteen-second mile.

'Some fine night,' says Tim, 'we'll be even with that clock's Master.'

'He's coming now,' says George, over his shoulder. 'I'm chasing the night west.'

The stars ahead dim no more than if a film of mist had been drawn under unobserved, but the deep air-boom on our skin changes to a joyful shout.

'The dawn-gust,' says Tim. 'It'll go on to meet the Sun. Look! Look! There's the dark

K

being crammed back over our bows! Come to the after-colloid. I'll show you something.'

The engine-room is hot and stuffy; the clerks in the coach are asleep, and the Slave of the Ray is ready to follow them. Tim slides open the aft colloid and reveals the curve of the world—the ocean's deepest purple—edged with fuming and intolerable gold. Then the Sun rises and through the colloid strikes out our lamps. Tim scowls in his face.

'Squirrels in a cage,' he mutters. 'That's all we are. Squirrels in a cage! He's going twice as fast as us. Just you wait a few years, my shining friend, and we'll take steps that will amaze you. *We*'ll Joshua you!'

Yes, that is our dream: to turn all earth into the Vale of Ajalon at our pleasure. So far, we can drag out the dawn to twice its normal length in these latitudes. But some day—even on the Equator—we shall hold the Sun level in his full stride.

Now we look down on a sea thronged with heavy traffic. A big submersible breaks water suddenly. Another and another follows with a swash and a suck and a savage bubbling of relieved pressures. The deep-sea freighters are rising to lung up after the long night, and the leisurely ocean is all patterned with peacock's eyes of foam.

'We'll lung up, too,' says Tim, and when we return to the c.p. George shuts off; the colloids are opened; and the fresh air sweeps her out. There is no hurry. The old contracts (they will be revised at the end of the year) allow twelve hours for a run which any packet can put behind her in ten. So we breakfast in the arms of an easterly slant which pushes us along at a languid twenty.

To enjoy life, and tobacco, begin both on a sunny morning half a mile or so above the dappled Atlantic cloud-belts and after a volt-flurry which has cleared and tempered your nerves. While we discussed the thickening traffic with the superiority that comes of having a high level reserved to ourselves, we heard (and I for the first time) the morning hymn on a Hospital boat.

She was cloaked by a skein of ravelled fluff beneath us and we caught the chant before she rose into the sunlight. '*O ye Winds of God,*' sang the unseen voices: '*bless ye the Lord! Praise Him and magnify Him for ever!*'

We slid off our caps and joined in. When our shadow fell across her great open platforms they looked up and stretched out their hands neighbourly while they sang. We could see the doctors and the nurses and the white-button-like faces of the cot-patients. She passed slowly beneath us, heading northward, her hull, wet with the dews of the night, all ablaze in the sunshine. So took she the shadow of a cloud and vanished, her song continuing. '*O ye holy and humble men of heart, bless ye the Lord! Praise Him and magnify Him for ever.*'

' She's a public lunger or she wouldn't have been singing the *Benedicite*; and she's a Greenlander or she wouldn't have snow-blinds over her colloids,' said George at last. ' She'll be bound

for Frederikshavn or one of the Glacier sana-
toriums for a month. If she was an accident ward
she'd be hung up at the eight-thousand-foot level.
Yes—consumptives.'

'Funny how the new things are the old things.
I've read in books,' Tim answered, 'that savages
used to haul their sick and wounded up to the
tops of hills because microbes were fewer there.
We hoist 'em into sterilised air for a while. Same
idea. How much do the doctors say we've added
to the average life of a man?'

'Thirty years,' says George, with a twinkle in
his eye. 'Are we going to spend 'em all up here,
Tim?'

'Flap ahead, then. Flap ahead. Who's
hindering?' the senior captain laughed, as we
went in.

We held a good lift to clear the coastwise and
Continental shipping; and we had need of it.
Though our route is in no sense a populated one,
there is a steady trickle of traffic this way along.
We met Hudson Bay furriers out of the Great
Preserve, hurrying to make their departure from
Bonavista with sable and black fox for the in-
satiable markets. We over-crossed Keewatin
liners, small and cramped; but their captains,
who see no land between Trepassy and Blanco,
know what gold they bring back from West
Africa. Trans-Asiatic Directs, we met, soberly
ringing the world round the Fiftieth Meridian
at an honest seventy knots; and white-painted
Ackroyd & Hunt fruiters out of the south fled
beneath us, their ventilated hulls whistling like

Chinese kites. Their market is in the North among the northern sanatoria, where you can smell their grape-fruit and bananas across the cold snows. Argentine beef boats we sighted too, of enormous capacity and unlovely outline. They, too, feed the northern health stations in ice-bound ports where submersibles dare not rise.

Yellow-bellied ore-flats and Ungava petrol-tanks punted down leisurely out of the North, like strings of unfrightened wild duck. It does not pay to fly minerals and oil a mile farther than is necessary; but the risks of transhipping to submersibles in the ice-pack off Nain or Hebron are so great that these heavy freighters fly down to Halifax direct, and scent the air as they go. They are the biggest tramps aloft except the Athabasca grain-tubs. But these last, now that the wheat is moved, are busy, over the world's shoulder, timber-lifting in Siberia.

We held to the St. Lawrence (it is astonishing how the old water-ways still pull us children of the air), and followed his broad line of black between its drifting ice-blocks, all down the Park which the wisdom of our fathers—but every one knows the Quebec run.

We dropped to the Heights Receiving Towers twenty minutes ahead of time, and there hung at ease till the Yokohama Intermediate Packet could pull out and give us our proper slip. It was curious to watch the action of the holding-down clips all along the frosty river front as the boats cleared or came to rest. A big Hamburger was leaving Pont Levis, and her crew, unshipping the platform railings, began to sing ' Elsinore '—the oldest of our chanteys. You know it of course :—

> *Mother Rügen's tea-house on the Baltic—*
> *Forty couple waltzing on the floor !*
> *And you can watch my Ray,*
> *For I must go away*
> *And dance with Ella Sweyn at Elsinore !*

Then, while they sweated home the covering-plates :—

> *Nor-Nor-Nor-Nor-*
> *West from Sourabaya to the Baltic—*
> *Ninety knot an hour to the Skaw !*
> *Mother Rügen's tea-house on the Baltic*
> *And a dance with Ella Sweyn at Elsinore !*

The clips parted with a gesture of indignant dismissal, as though Quebec, glittering under her snows, were casting out these light and unworthy lovers. Our signal came from the Heights. Tim turned and floated up, but surely then it was with passionate appeal that the great tower arms flung open—or did I think so because on the upper staging a little hooded figure also opened her arms wide towards her father?

.   .   .   .   .

In ten seconds the coach with its clerks clashed down to the receiving-caisson ; the hostlers displaced the engineers at the idle turbines, and Tim, prouder of this than all, introduced me to the maiden of the photograph on the shelf. ' And by the way,' said he to her, stepping forth in sunshine under the hat of civil life, ' I saw young Williams in the Mark Boat. I've asked him to tea on Friday.'

AERIAL BOARD OF CONTROL

Lights

No changes in English Inland lights for week ending Dec. 18th.

CAPE VERDE. Week ending Dec. 18th. Verde inclined guide - light changes from 1st proximo to triple flash—green white green—in place of occulting red as heretofore. The warning light for Harmattan winds will be continuous vertical glare (white) on all oases of trans-Saharan N.E. by E. Main Routes.

INVERCARGILL (N.Z.)—From 1st prox.: extreme southerly light (double red) will exhibit white beam inclined 45 degrees on approach of Southerly Buster. Traffic flies high off this coast between April and October.

TABLE BAY—Devil's Peak Glare removed to Simonsberg. Traffic making Table Mountain coastwise keep all lights from Three Anchor Bay at least two thousand feet under, and do not round to till East of E. shoulder Devil's Peak.

SANDHEADS LIGHT—Green triple vertical marks new private landing-stage for Bay and Burma traffic only.

SNAEFELL JOKUL—White occulting light withdrawn for winter.

PATAGONIA—No summer light south Cape Pilar. This includes Staten Island and Port Stanley.

C. NAVARIN—Quadruple fog flash (white), one minute intervals (new).

EAST CAPE—Fog flash—single white with single bomb, 30 sec. intervals (new).

MALAYAN ARCHIPELAGO lights unreliable owing eruptions. Lay from Cape Somerset to Singapore direct, keeping highest levels.

For the Board:

CATTERTHUN
ST. JUST   } *Lights.*
VAN HEDDER

Casualties

Week ending Dec. 18th.

SABLE ISLAND—Green single-barbette tower freighter, number indistinguishable, up-ended, and fore-tank pierced after collision, passed 300-ft. level 2 P.M. Dec. 15th. Watched to water and pithed by Mark Boat.

N.F. BANKS—Postal Packet 162 reports *Halma* freighter (Fowey — St. John's) abandoned, leaking after weather, 46° 15′ N. 50° 15′ W. Crew rescued by Planet liner *Asteroid.* Watched to water and pithed by Postal Packet, Dec. 14th.

KERGUELEN MARK BOAT reports last call from *Cymena* freighter (Gayer Tong Huk & Co.) taking water and sinking in snow-storm South McDonald Islands. No wreckage recovered. Messages and wills of crew at all A.B.C. offices.

FEZZAN—T.A.D. freighter *Ulema* taken ground during Harmattan on Akakus Range. Under plates strained. Crew at Ghat where repairing Dec. 13th.

BISCAY, MARK BOAT reports *Carducci* (Valandingham Line) slightly spiked in western gorge Pointe de

Benasque. Passengers transferred *Andorra* (Fulton Line). Barcelona Mark Boat salving cargo Dec. 12th.

ASCENSION, MARK BOAT—Wreck of unknown racing-plane, Parden rudder, wire-stiffened xylonite vans, and Harliss engine-seating, sighted and salved 7° 20' S. 18° 41' W. Dec. 15th. Photos at all A.B.C. offices.

Missing

No answer to General Call having been received during the last week from following overdues, they are posted as missing :—

Atlantis, W. 17630	.	Canton—Valparaiso
Audhumla, W. 889	.	Stockholm—Odessa
Berenice, W. 2206	.	Riga—Vladivostock
Draco, E. 446 .	.	Coventry—Puntas Arenas
Tontine, E. 3068	.	C. Wrath—Ungava
Wu-Sung, E. 41776	.	Hankow—Lobito Bay

General Call (all Mark Boats) out for :—

Jane Eyre, W. 6990	.	Port Rupert—City of Mexico
Santander, W. 5514	.	Gobi Desert—Manila
V. Edmundsun, E. 9690	.	Kandahar—Fiume

Broke for Obstruction, and Quitting Levels

VALKYRIE (racing plane), A. J. Hartley owner, New York (twice warned).

GEISHA (racing plane), S. van Cott owner, Philadelphia (twice warned).

MARVEL OF PERU (racing plane), J. X. Peixoto owner, Rio de Janeiro (twice warned).

For the Board:

LAZAREFF
McKEOUGH }*Traffic.*
GOLDBLATT

NOTES

High-Level Sleet

The Northern weather so far shows no sign of improvement. From all quarters come complaints of the unusual prevalence of sleet at the higher levels. Racing-planes and digs alike have suffered severely—the former from unequal deposits of half-frozen slush on their vans (and only those who have ' held up ' a badly balanced plane in a cross-wind know what that means), and the latter from loaded bows and snow-cased bodies. As a consequence, the Northern and North-western upper levels have been practically abandoned, and the high fliers have returned to the ignoble security of the Three, Five, and Six thousand foot levels. But there remain a few undaunted sun-hunters who, in spite of frozen stays and ice-jammed connecting-rods, still haunt the blue empyrean.

Bat-Boat Racing

The scandals of the past few years have at last moved the yachting world to concerted action in regard to ' bat '-boat racing.

We have been treated to the spectacle of what are practically keeled racing-planes driven a clear five foot or more above the water, and only eased down to touch their so-called ' native element ' as they near the line. Judges and starters have been conveniently blind to this absurdity, but the public demonstration off St. Catherine's Light at the Autumn Regattas has borne ample, if tardy, fruit. In future the 'bat' is to be a boat, and the long-unheeded demand of the true sportsman for 'no daylight under mid-keel in smooth water' is in a fair way to be conceded. The new rule severely restricts plane area and lift alike. The gas compartments are permitted both fore and aft, as in the old type, but the water-ballast central tank is rendered obligatory. These things work, if not for perfection, at least for the evolution of a sane and whole-some *water-borne* cruiser. The type of rudder is unaffected by the new rules, so we may expect to see the Long-Davidson make (the patent on which has just expired) come largely into use henceforward, though the strain on the sternpost in turning at speeds over sixty miles an hour is admittedly very severe. But bat-boat racing has a great future before it.

Crete and the A.B.C.

The story of the recent Cretan crisis, as told in the *A.B.C. Monthly Report*, is not without humour. Till 25th October Crete, as all the planet knows, was the sole surviving European repository of 'autonomous institu-tions,' 'local self-government,' and the rest of the archaic lumber devised in the past for the confusion of human affairs. She has lived practically on the tourist traffic attracted by her annual pageants of Parliaments, Boards, Municipal Councils, etc. etc. Last summer the islanders grew wearied, as their Premier explained, of 'playing at being savages for pennies,' and proceeded to pull down all the landing-towers on the island and shut off general communication till such time as the A.B.C. should annex them. For side-splitting comedy we would refer our readers to the correspondence between the Board of Control and the Cretan Premier during the 'war.' However, all's well that ends well. The A.B.C. have taken over the administration of Crete on normal lines; and tourists must go elsewhere to witness the ' debates,' ' resolutions,' and ' popular movements ' of the old days.   The only people who suffer will be the Board of Control, which is grievously overworked already.   It is easy enough to condemn the Cretans for their laziness; but when one recalls the large, prosperous, and presumably public-spirited communities which during the last few years have deliberately thrown themselves into the hands of the A.B.C., one cannot be too hard upon St. Paul's old friends.

CORRESPONDENCE

Skylarking on the Equator

To THE EDITOR—Only last week, while crossing the Equator (W. 26·15), I became aware of a furious and irregular cannonading some fifteen or twenty knots S. 4 E. Descending to the 5000 ft. level, I found a party of Transylvanian tourists engaged in exploding scores of the largest pattern atmospheric bombs (A.B.C. standard) and, in the intervals of their pleasing labours, firing bow and stern smoke-ring swivels. This orgy—I can give it no other name—went on for at least two hours, and naturally produced violent electric derangements. My compasses, of course, were thrown out, my bow was struck twice, and I received two brisk shocks from the lower platform-rail. On remonstrating, I was told that these ' professors ' were engaged in scientific experiments. The extent of their ' scientific ' knowledge may be judged by the fact that they expected to produce (I give their own words) ' a little blue sky ' if ' they went on long enough.' This in the heart of the Doldrums at 4500 feet ! I have no objection to any amount of blue sky in its proper place (it can be found at the 4000 level for practically twelve months out of the year), but I submit, with all deference to the educational needs of Transylvania, that ' skylarking ' in the centre of a main-travelled road where, at the best of times, electricity literally drips off one's stanchions and screw-blades, is unnecessary. When my friends had finished, the road was seamed and blown and pitted with unequal

pressure-layers, spirals, vortices, and readjustments for at
least an hour.   I pitched badly twice in an upward rush—
solely due to these diabolical throw-downs—that came
near to wrecking my propeller.   Equatorial work at low
levels is trying enough in all conscience without the added
terrors of scientific hooliganism in the Doldrums.

Rhyl.   J. VINCENT MATHEN.

[We entirely sympathise with Professor Mathen's
views, but till the Board sees fit to further regulate the
Southern areas in which scientific experiments may be
conducted, we shall always be exposed to the risk which
our correspondent describes.   Unfortunately, a chimera
bombinating in a vacuum is, nowadays, only too capable of
producing secondary causes.—*Editor*.]

Answers to Correspondents

VIGILANS—The Laws of Auroral Derangements are
still imperfectly understood.   Any overheated motor may
of course 'seize' without warning ;   but so many complaints have reached us of accidents similar to yours while
shooting the Aurora that we are inclined to believe with
Lavalle that the upper strata of the Aurora Borealis are
practically one big electric 'leak,' and that the paralysis of
your engines was due to complete magnetisation of all
metallic parts.   Low-flying planes often 'glue up' when
near the Magnetic Pole, and there is no reason in science
why the same disability should not be experienced at higher
levels when the Auroras are 'delivering' strongly.

INDIGNANT—On your own showing, you were not
under control.   That you could not hoist the necessary
N.U.C. lights on approaching a traffic-lane because your
electrics had short-circuited is a misfortune which might
befall any one.   The A.B.C., being responsible for the
planet's traffic, cannot, however, make allowance for this
kind of misfortune.   A reference to the Code will show
that you were fined on the lower scale.

PLANISTON—(1) The Five Thousand Kilometre (overland) was won last year by L. V. Rautsch ; R. M. Rautsch, his brother, in the same week pulling off the Ten Thousand (oversea). R. M.'s average worked out at a fraction over 700 kilometres per hour, thus constituting a record. (2) Theoretically, there is no limit to the lift of a dirigible. For commercial and practical purposes 15,000 tons is accepted as the most manageable.

PATERFAMILIAS—None whatever. He is liable for both direct damage to your chimneys and any collateral damage caused by fall of bricks into garden, etc. etc. Bodily inconvenience and mental anguish may be included, but the average courts are not, as a rule, swayed by sentiment. If you can prove that his grapnel removed *any* portion of your roof, you had better rest your case on decoverture of domicile (See Parkins *v.* Duboulay). We sympathise with your position, but the night of the 14th was stormy and confused, and—you may have to anchor on a stranger's chimney yourself some night. *Verbum sap.!*

ALDEBARAN—(1) War, as a paying concern, ceased in 1967. (2) The Convention of London expressly reserves to every nation the right of waging war so long as it does not interfere with traffic and all that it implies. (3) The A.B.C. was constituted in 1949.

L. M. D.—Keep her full head-on at half power, taking advantage of the lulls to speed up and creep into it. She will strain much less this way than in quartering across a gale. (2) Nothing is to be gained by reversing into a following gale, and there is always risk of a turnover. (3) The formulae for stuns'l brakes are uniformly unreliable, and will continue to be so as long as air is compressible.

PEGAMOID—Personally we prefer glass or flux compounds to any other material for winter-work nose-caps as being absolutely non-hygroscopic. (2) We cannot recommend any particular make.

PULMONAR—For the symptoms you describe, try the

Gobi Desert Sanatoria. The low levels of most of the Saharan Sanatoria are against them except at the outset of the disease. (2) We do not recommend boarding-houses or hotels in this column.

BEGINNER—On still days the air above a large inhabited city being slightly warmer—*i.e.*, thinner—than the atmosphere of the surrounding country, a plane drops a little on entering the rarefied area, precisely as a ship sinks a little in fresh water. Hence the phenomena of 'jolt' and your 'inexplicable collisions' with factory chimneys. In air, as on earth, it is safest to fly high.

EMERGENCY—There is only one rule of the road in air, earth, and water. Do you want the firmament to yourself?

PICCIOLA—Both Poles have been overdone in Art and Literature. Leave them to Science for the next twenty years. You did not send a stamp with your verses.

NORTH NIGERIA—The Mark Boat was within her right in warning you off the Reserve. The shadow of a low-flying dirigible scares the game. You can buy all the photos you need at Sokoto.

NEW ERA—It is not etiquette to overcross an A.B.C. official's boat without asking permission. He is one of the body responsible for the planet's traffic, and for that reason must not be interfered with. You, presumably, are out on your own business or pleasure, and must leave him alone. For humanity's sake don't try to be 'democratic.'

EXCORIATED—All inflators chafe sooner or later. You must go on till your skin hardens by practice. Meantime vaseline.

REVIEW

The Life of Xavier Lavalle

(Reviewed by René Talland. École Aéronautique, Paris)

Ten years ago Lavalle, 'that imperturbable dreamer
of the heavens,' as Lazareff hailed him, gathered together
the fruits of a lifetime's labour, and gave it, with well-
justified contempt, to a world bound hand and foot to
Barald's Theory of Vertices and 'compensating electric
nodes.' 'They shall see,' he wrote,—in that immortal
postscript to *The Heart of the Cyclone*—'the Laws whose
existence they derided written in fire *beneath* them.'

'But even here,' he continues, 'there is no finality.
Better a thousand times my conclusions should be dis-
credited than that my dead name should lie across the
threshold of the temple of Science—a bar to further
inquiry.'

So died Lavalle—a prince of the Powers of the Air,
and even at his funeral Cellier jested at 'him who had
gone to discover the secrets of the Aurora Borealis.'

If I choose thus to be banal, it is only to remind you
that Cellier's theories are to-day as exploded as the
ludicrous deductions of the Spanish school. In the place
of their fugitive and warring dreams we have, definitely,
Lavalle's Law of the Cyclone which he surprised in darkness and cold at the foot of the overarching throne of the
Aurora Borealis. It is there that I, intent on my own
investigations, have passed and re-passed a hundred times

L

the worn leonine face, white as the snow beneath him,
furrowed with wrinkles like the seams and gashes upon the
North Cape ; the nervous hand, integrally a part of the
mechanism of his flighter ; and above all, the wonderful
lambent eyes turned to the zenith.

' Master,' I would cry as I moved respectfully beneath
him, ' what is it you seek to-day ? ' and always the answer,
clear and without doubt, from above :   ' The old secret,
my son ! '

The immense egotism of youth forced me on my own
path, but (cry of the human always !) had I known—if I
had known—I would many times have bartered my poor
laurels for the privilege, such as Tinsley and Herrera
possess, of having aided him in his monumental researches.

It is to the filial piety of Victor Lavalle that we owe
the two volumes consecrated to the ground-life of his
father, so full of the holy intimacies of the domestic hearth.
Once returned from the abysms of the utter North to that
little house upon the outskirts of Meudon, it was not the
philosopher, the daring observer, the man of iron energy
that imposed himself on his family, but a fat and even
plaintive jester, a farceur incarnate and kindly, the co-
equal of his children, and, it must be written, not seldom
the comic despair of Madame Lavalle, who, as she writes
five years after the marriage, to her venerable mother,
found ' in this unequalled intellect whose name I bear the
abandon of a large and very untidy boy.' Here is her letter :

' Xavier returned from I do not know where at midnight, absorbed in calculations on the eternal question of
his Aurora—*la belle Aurore*, whom I begin to hate.
Instead of anchoring—I had set out the guide-light above
our roof, so he had but to descend and fasten the plane—
he wandered, profoundly distracted, above the town with
his anchor down ! Figure to yourself, dear mother, it is
the roof of the mayor's house that the grapnel first engages !
That I do not regret, for the mayor's wife and I are not
sympathetic ; but when Xavier uproots my pet araucaria
and bears it across the garden into the conservatory I

protest at the top of my voice. Little Victor in his night-clothes runs to the window, enormously amused at the parabolic flight without reason, for it is too dark to see the grapnel, of my prized tree. The Mayor of Meudon thunders at our door in the name of the Law, demanding, I suppose, my husband's head. Here is the conversation through the megaphone—Xavier is two hundred feet above us.

' " Monsieur Lavalle, descend and make reparation for outrage of domicile. Descend, Monsieur Lavalle ! "

' No one answers.

' " Xavier Lavalle, in the name of the Law, descend and submit to process for outrage of domicile."

' Xavier, roused from his calculations, only compre-hending the last words : " Outrage of domicile ? My dear mayor, who is the man that has corrupted thy Julie ? "

' The mayor, furious, " Xavier Lavalle―― "

' Xavier, interrupting : " I have not that felicity. I am only a dealer in cyclones ! "

' My faith, he raised one then ! All Meudon attended in the streets, and my Xavier, after a long time compre-hending what he had done, excused himself in a thousand apologies. At last the reconciliation was effected in our house over a supper at two in the morning—Julie in a wonderful costume of compromises, and I have her and the mayor pacified in bed in the blue room.'

And on the next day, while the mayor rebuilds his roof, her Xavier departs anew for the Aurora Borealis, there to commence his life's work. M. Victor Lavalle tells us of that historic collision (*en plane*) on the flank of Hecla between Herrera, then a pillar of the Spanish school, and the man destined to confute his theories and lead him intellectually captive. Even through the years, the im-mense laugh of Lavalle as he sustains the Spaniard's wrecked plane, and cries : ' Courage ! *I* shall not fall till I have found Truth, and I hold *you* fast ! ' rings like the call of trumpets. This is that Lavalle whom the world, immersed in speculations of immediate gain, did not know or suspect—the Lavalle whom they judged to the last a pedant and a theorist.

The human, as apart from the scientific, side (developed in his own volumes) of his epoch-making discoveries is marked with a simplicity, clarity, and good sense beyond praise. I would specially refer such as doubt the sustaining influence of ancestral faith upon character and will to the eleventh and nineteenth chapters, in which are contained the opening and consummation of the Tellurionical Records extending over nine years. Of their tremendous significance be sure that the modest house at Meudon knew as little as that the Records would one day be the planet's standard in all official meteorology. It was enough for them that their Xavier—this son, this father, this husband—ascended periodically to commune with powers, it might be angelic, beyond their comprehension, and that they united daily in prayers for his safety.

'Pray for me,' he says upon the eve of each of his excursions, and returning, with an equal simplicity, he renders thanks 'after supper in the little room where he kept his barometers.'

To the last Lavalle was a Catholic of the old school, accepting—he who had looked into the very heart of the lightnings—the dogmas of papal infallibility, of absolution, of confession—of relics great and small. Marvellous—enviable contradiction!

The completion of the Tellurionical Records closed what Lavalle himself was pleased to call the theoretical side of his labours—labours from which the youngest and least impressionable planeur might well have shrunk. He had traced through cold and heat, across the deeps of the oceans, with instruments of his own invention, over the inhospitable heart of the polar ice and the sterile visage of the deserts, league by league, patiently, unweariedly, remorselessly, from their ever-shifting cradle under the magnetic pole to their exalted death-bed in the utmost ether of the upper atmosphere—each one of the Isoconical Tellurions—Lavalle's Curves, as we call them to-day.

He had disentangled the nodes of their intersections, assigning to each its regulated period of flux and reflux. Thus equipped, he summons Herrera and Tinsley, his pupils, to the final demonstration as calmly as though he were ordering his flighter for some mid-day journey to Marseilles.

' I have proved my thesis,' he writes. ' It remains now only that you should witness the proof. We go to Manila to-morrow. A cyclone will form off the Pescadores S. 17 E. in four days, and will reach its maximum intensity twenty-seven hours after inception. It is there I will show you the Truth.'

A letter heretofore unpublished from Herrera to Madame Lavalle tells us how the Master's prophecy was verified.

I will not destroy its simplicity or its significance by any attempt to quote. Note well, though, that Herrera's preoccupation throughout that day and night of superhuman strain is always for the Master's bodily health and comfort. ' At such a time,' he writes, ' I forced the Master to take the broth ' ; or ' I made him put on the fur coat as you told me.' Nor is Tinsley (see pp. 184-85) less concerned. He prepares the nourishment. He cooks eternally, imperturbably, suspended in the chaos of which the Master interprets the meaning. Tinsley, bowed down with the laurels of both hemispheres, raises himself to yet nobler heights in his capacity of a devoted *chef*. It is almost unbelievable ! And yet men write of the Master as cold, aloof, self-contained. Such characters do not elicit the joyous and unswerving devotion which Lavalle commanded throughout life. Truly, we have changed very little in the course of the ages ! The secrets of earth and sky and the links that bind them, we felicitate ourselves we are on the road to discover ; but our neighbour's heart and mind we misread, we misjudge, we condemn—now as ever. Let all then who love a man read these most human, tender, and wise volumes !

Miscellaneous

WANTS

REQUIRED IMMEDIATELY, for East Africa, a thoroughly competent Plane and Dirigible Driver, acquainted with Radium and Helium motors and generators. Low-level work only, but must understand heavyweight digs.

MOSSAMEDES TRANSPORT ASSOC.
84 Palestine Buildings, E.C.

MAN WANTED—DIG DRIVER for Southern Alps with Saharan summer trips. High levels, high speed, high wages.

Apply M. SIDNEY,
Hotel San Stefano, Monte Carlo.

FAMILY DIRIGIBLE. A COMpetent, steady man wanted for slow-speed, low-level Tangye dirigible. No night work, no sea trips. Must be member of the Church of England, and make himself useful in the garden.

M. R.,
The Rectory, Gray's Barton, Wilts.

COMMERCIAL DIG, CENTRAL and Southern Europe. A smart, active man for a L.M.T. Dig. Night work only. Headquarters London and Cairo. Linguist preferred.

BAGMAN,
Charing Cross Hotel, W.C.

FOR SALE — A BARGAIN — Single Plane, narrow-gauge vans, Pinke motor. Restayed this autumn. Hansen air-kit, 38 in. chest, 15½ collar. Can be seen by appointment.

N. 2650. This office.

The Bee-Line Bookshop

BELT'S WAY-BOOKS, giving town lights for all towns over 4000 pop. as laid down by A.B.C.

THE WORLD. Complete 2 vols. Thin Oxford, limp back. 12s. 6d.

BELT'S COASTAL ITINERARY. Shore Lights of the World. 7s. 6d.

THE TRANSATLANTIC AND MEDITERRANEAN TRAFFIC LINES. (By authority of the A.B.C.) Paper, 1s. 6d. ; cloth, 2s. 6d. Ready Jan. 15.

ARCTIC AEROPLANING. Siemens and Galt. Cloth, bds. 3s. 6d.

LAVALLE'S HEART OF THE CYCLONE, with supplementary charts. 4s 6d.

RIMINGTON'S PITFALLS IN THE AIR, and Table of Comparative Densities. 3s. 6d.

ANGELO'S DESERT IN A DIRIGIBLE. New edition, revised. 5s. 9d.

VAUGHAN'S PLANE RACING IN CALM AND STORM. 2s. 6d.

VAUGHAN'S HINTS TO THE AIRMATEUR. 1s.

HOFMAN'S LAWS OF LIFT AND VELOCITY. With diagrams, 3s. 6d.

DE VITRE'S THEORY OF SHIFTING BALLAST IN DIRIGIBLES. 2s. 6d.

SANGER'S WEATHERS OF THE WORLD. 4s.

SANGER'S TEMPERATURES AT HIGH ALTITUDES. 4s.

HAWKIN'S FOG AND HOW TO AVOID IT. 3s.

VAN ZUYLAN'S SECONDARY EFFECTS OF THUNDERSTORMS. 4s. 6d.

DAHLGREN'S AIR CURRENTS AND EPIDEMIC DISEASES. 5s. 6d.

REDMAYNE'S DISEASE AND THE BAROMETER 7s. 6d.

WALTON'S HEALTH RESORTS OF THE GOBI AND SHAMO. 3s. 6d.

WALTON'S THE POLE AND PULMONARY COMPLAINTS. 7s. 6d.

MUTLOW'S HIGH LEVEL BACTERIOLOGY. 7s. 6d.

HALLIWELL'S ILLUMINATED STAR MAP, with clockwork attachment, giving apparent motion of heavens, boxed, complete with clamps for binnacle, 36 inch size only, £2:2s. (Invaluable for night work.) With A.B.C. certificate, £3:10s.

ZALINSKI'S Standard Works :
  PASSES OF THE HIMALAYAS. 5s.
  PASSES OF THE SIERRAS. 5s.
  PASSES OF THE ROCKIES. 5s.
  PASSES OF THE URALS. 5s.
  The four boxed, limp cloth, with charts, 15s.

GRAY'S AIR CURRENTS IN MOUNTAIN GORGES. 7s. 6d.

A. C. BELT & SON, READING

Bat=Boats

Flint & Mantel
Southampton

FOR SALE

at the end of Season the following Bat-Boats:

GRISELDA, 65 knt., 42 ft., 430 (nom.) Maginnis Motor, under-rake rudder.

MABELLE, 50 knt., 40 ft., 310 Hargreaves Motor, Douglas' lock-steering gear.

IVEMONA, 50 knt., 35 ft., 300 Hargreaves (Radium accelerator), Miller keel and rudder.

The above are well known on the South Coast as sound, wholesome knockabout boats, with ample cruising accommodation. *Griselda* carries spare set of Hofman racing vans, and can be lifted three foot clear in smooth water with ballast-tank swung aft. The others do not lift clear, and are recommended for beginners.

Also, by private treaty, racing B.B. *Tarpon* (76 winning flags) 120 knt., 60 ft.; Long-Davidson double under-rake rudder, new this season and unstrained. 850 nom. Maginnis motor, Radium relays and Pond generator. Bronze breakwater forward, and treble reinforced forefoot and entry. Talfourd rockered keel. Triple set of Hofman vans, giving maximum lifting surface of 5327 sq. ft.

Tarpon has been lifted *and held* seven feet for four miles between touch and touch.

Our Autumn List of racing and family Bats ready on the 9th January.

CHRISTIAN WR

ESTABLIS

Accessories

Hooded Binnacles with dip-dials automatically recording change of level (illuminated face).

All heights from 50 to 18,000 feet	£2	10	0
With Aerial Board of Control certificate	£3	11	0

Foot and Hand Fog-horns; Sirens toned to any club note; with air-chest, belt-driven from motor £6 8 0

Wireless installations syntonised to A.B.C. requirements, in neat mahogany case, hundred mile range £3 3 0

Grapnels, mushroom anchors, pithing-irons, winches, hawsers, snaps, shackles, and mooring ropes, for lawn, city, and public installations.

Detachable under-cars, aluminium or stamped steel.

Keeled under-cars for planes: single-action detaching-gear, turning car into boat with one motion of the wrist. Invaluable for sea trips.

Head, side, and riding lights (by size) Nos. 00 to 20 A.B.C. Standard. Rockets and fog-bombs in colours and tones of the principal clubs (boxed).

A selection of twenty	£2	17	6
International night-signals (boxed)	£1	11	6

Catalogues free th

IGHT & OLDIS

HED 1924

and Spares

Spare generators guaranteed to lifting power marked on cover (prices according to power).

Wind-noses for dirigibles—Pegamoid, cane-stiffened, lacquered cane or aluminium and flux for winter work.

Smoke-ring cannon for hail-storms, swivel-mounted, bow or stern.

Propeller-blades: metal, tungsten backed; papier-mâché, wire stiffened; ribbed xylonite (Nickson's patent); all razor-edged (price by pitch and diameter).

Compressed steel bow-screws for winter work.

Fused Ruby or Commercial Mineral Co. bearings and collars. Agate-mounted thrust-blocks up to 4 inch.

Magniac's bow-rudders—(Lavalle's patent grooving).

Wove steel beltings for outboard motors (non-magnetic).

Radium batteries, all powers to 150 h.p. (in pairs).

Helium batteries, all powers to 300 h.p. (tandem).

Stuns'l brakes worked from upper or lower platform.

Direct plunge-brakes worked from lower platform only, loaded silk or fibre, wind-tight.

ughout the Planet

THE FOUR ANGELS

As Adam lay a-dreaming beneath the Apple Tree,
The Angel of the Earth came down, and offered Earth in fee.
   But Adam did not need it,
   Nor the plough he would not speed it,
  Singing :—' Earth and Water, Air and Fire,
     What more can mortal man desire ? '
     (The Apple Tree's in bud.)

As Adam lay a-dreaming beneath the Apple Tree,
The Angel of the Waters offered all the Seas in fee.
   But Adam would not take 'em,
   Nor the ships he wouldn't make 'em,
  Singing :—' Water, Earth and Air and Fire,
     What more can mortal man desire ? '
     (The Apple Tree's in leaf.)

As Adam lay a-dreaming beneath the Apple Tree,
The Angel of the Air he offered all the Air in fee.
   But Adam did not crave it,
   Nor the voyage he wouldn't brave it,
  Singing :—' Air and Water, Earth and Fire,
     What more can mortal man desire ? '
     (The Apple Tree's in bloom.)

As Adam lay a-dreaming beneath the Apple Tree,
The Angel of the Fire rose up and not a word said he.
   But he wished a Fire and made it,
   And in Adam's heart he laid it,
  Singing :—' Fire, Fire, burning Fire,
     Stand up and reach your heart's desire ? '
     (The Apple Blossom's set.)

As Adam was a-working outside of Eden-Wall,
He used the Earth, he used the Seas, he used the Air and all ;
   And out of black disaster
   He arose to be the master
    Of Earth and Water, Air and Fire,
    But never reached his heart's desire !
     (The Apple Tree's cut down !)

A Deal in Cotton

A Deal in Cotton

Long and long ago, when Devadatta was King of Benares, I wrote some tales concerning Strickland of the Punjab Police (who married Miss Youghal), and Adam, his son. Strickland has finished his Indian service, and lives now at a place in England called Weston-super-Mare, where his wife plays the organ in one of the churches. Semi-occasionally he comes up to London, and occasionally his wife makes him visit his friends. Otherwise he plays golf and follows the harriers for his figure's sake.

If you remember that Infant who told a tale to Eustace Cleever the novelist, you will remember that he became a baronet with a vast estate. He has, owing to cookery, a little lost his figure, but he never loses his friends. I have found a wing of his house turned into a hospital for sick men, and there I once spent a week in the company of two dismal nurses and a specialist in 'Sprue.' Another time the place was full of schoolboys— sons of Anglo-Indians—whom The Infant had collected for the holidays, and they nearly broke his keeper's heart.

But my last visit was better. The Infant called

me up by wire, and I fell into the arms of a friend of mine, Colonel A. L. Corkran, so that the years departed from us, and we praised Allah, who had not yet terminated the Delights, nor separated the Companions.

Said Corkran, when he had explained how it felt to command a native Infantry regiment on the Border : ' The Stricks are coming for to-night —with their boy.'

' I remember him. The little fellow I wrote a story about,' I said. ' Is he in the Service ? '

' No. Strick got him into the Centro-Euro-Africo Protectorate. He's Assistant-Commissioner at Dupé—wherever that is. Somaliland, ain't it, Stalky ? ' asked The Infant.

Stalky puffed out his nostrils scornfully. ' You're only three thousand miles out. Look at the atlas.'

' Anyhow, he's as rotten full of fever as the rest of you,' said The Infant, at length on the big divan.   ' And he's bringing a native servant with him. Stalky, be an athlete, and tell Ipps to put him in the stable room.'

' Why? Is he a Yao—like the fellow Wade brought here—when your housekeeper had fits ? ' Stalky often visits The Infant, and has seen some odd things.

' No. He's one of old Strickland's Punjabi policemen—and quite European—I believe.'

' Hooray ! Haven't talked Punjabi for three months—and a Punjabi from Central Africa ought to be amusin'.'

We heard the chuff of the motor in the porch,

and the first to enter was Agnes Strickland, whom
The Infant makes no secret of adoring.

He is devoted, in a fat man's placid way, to at
least eight designing women; but she nursed him
once through a bad bout of Peshawur fever, and
when she is in his house, it is more than all hers.

'You didn't send rugs enough,' she began.
'Adam might have taken a chill.'

'It's quite warm in the car. Why did you let
him ride in front?'

'Because he wanted to,' she replied, with the
mother's smile, and we were introduced to the
shadow of a young man leaning heavily on the
shoulder of a bearded Punjabi Mohammedan.

'This is all that came home of him,' said his
father to me. There was nothing in it of the child
with whom I had journeyed to Dalhousie centuries
since.

'And what is this uniform?' Stalky asked of
Imam Din, the servant, who came to attention on
the marble floor.

'The uniform of the Protectorate troops,
Sahib. Though I am the Little Sahib's body-
servant, it is not seemly for us white men to be
attended by folk dressed altogether as servants.'

'And—and we white men wait at table on
horseback?' Stalky pointed to the man's spurs.

'These I added for the sake of honour when I
came to England,' said Imam Din.

Adam smiled the ghost of a little smile that I
began to remember, and we put him on the big
couch for refreshments. Stalky asked him how
much leave he had, and he said: 'Six months.'

'But he'll take another six on medical certificate,' said Agnes anxiously. Adam knit his brows.

'You don't want to—eh? *I* know. Wonder what *my* second in command is doing.' Stalky tugged his moustache, and fell to thinking of his Sikhs.

'Ah!' said The Infant. 'I've only a few thousand pheasants to look after. Come along and dress for dinner. We're just ourselves. What flowers is your honour's ladyship commanding for the table?'

'Just ourselves?' she said, looking at the crotons in the great hall. 'Then let's have marigolds—the little cemetery ones.'

So it was ordered.

Now, marigolds to us mean hot weather, discomfort, parting, and death. That smell in our nostrils, and Adam's servant in waiting, we naturally fell back more and more on the old slang, recalling at each glass those who had gone before. We did not sit at the big table, but in the bay-window overlooking the park, where they were carting the last of the hay. When twilight fell we would not have candles, but waited for the moon, and continued our talk in the dusk that makes one remember.

Young Adam was not interested in our past except where it had touched his future. I think his mother held his hand beneath the table. Imam Din—shoeless, out of respect to the floors —brought him his medicine, poured it drop by drop, and asked for orders.

' Wait to take him to his cot when he grows weary,' said his mother, and Imam Din retired into the shadow by the ancestral portraits.

' Now what d'you expect to get *out* of your country?' The Infant asked, when—our India laid aside—we talked Adam's Africa. It roused him at once.

' Rubber—nuts—gums—and so on,' he said. ' But our real future is cotton. I grew fifty acres of it last year in my District.'

' My District!' said his father. ' Hear him, Mummy!'

' I did, though! I wish I could show you the sample. Some Manchester chaps said it was as good as any Sea Island cotton on the market.'

' But what made you a cotton-planter, my son?' she asked.

' My Chief said every man ought to have a *shouk* [a hobby] of sorts, and he took the trouble to ride a day out of his way to show me a belt of black soil that was just the thing for cotton.'

' Ah! What was your Chief like?' Stalky asked, in his silkiest tones.

' The best man alive—absolutely. He lets you blow your own nose yourself. The people call him '—Adam jerked out some heathen phrase—' that means the Man with the Stone Eyes, you know.'

' I'm glad of that. Because I've heard—from other quarters '——Stalky's sentence burned like a slow match, but the explosion was not long delayed.

' Other quarters!' Adam threw out a thin

hand. ' Every dog has his fleas. If you listen to
them, of course ! ' The shake of his head was as
I remembered it among his father's policemen
twenty years before, and his mother's eyes shining
through the dusk called on me to adore it. I
kicked Stalky on the shin. One must not mock
a young man's first love or loyalty.

A lump of raw cotton appeared on the table.

' I thought there might be a need. Therefore
I packed it between our shirts,' said the voice of
Imam Din.

' Does he know as much English as that ? ' cried
The Infant, who had forgotten his East.

We all admired the cotton for Adam's sake,
and, indeed, it was very long and glossy.

' It's—it's only an experiment,' he said.
' We're such awful paupers we can't even pay for
a mail-cart in my District. We use a biscuit-box
on two bicycle wheels. I only got the money for
that '—he patted the stuff—' by a pure fluke.'

' How much did it cost ? ' asked Strickland.

' With seed and machinery—about two hundred
pounds. I had the labour done by cannibals.'

' That sounds promising.' Stalky reached for
a fresh cigarette.

' No, thank you,' said Agnes. ' I've been at
Weston-super-Mare a little too long for cannibals.
I'll go to the music-room and try over next
Sunday's hymns.'

She lifted the boy's hand lightly to her lips,
and tripped across the acres of glimmering floor
to the music-room that had been The Infant's
ancestors' banqueting-hall. Her grey and silver

dress disappeared under the musicians' gallery;
two electrics broke out, and she stood backed
against the lines of gilded pipes.

'There's an abominable self-playing attachment here!' she called.

'Me!' The Infant answered, his napkin on
his shoulder. 'That's how I play *Parsifal*.'

'I prefer the direct expression. Take it away,
Ipps.'

We heard old Ipps skating obediently all over
the floor.

'Now for the direct expression,' said Stalky,
and moved on the Burgundy recommended by the
faculty to enrich fever-thinned blood.

'It's nothing much. Only the belt of cotton-
soil my Chief showed me ran right into the
Sheshaheli country. We haven't been able to
prove cannibalism against that tribe in the courts;
but when a Sheshaheli offers you four pounds of
woman's breast, tattoo-marks and all, skewered
up in a plantain leaf before breakfast, you——'

'Naturally burn the villages before lunch,' said
Stalky.

Adam shook his head. 'No troops,' he sighed.
'I told my Chief about it, and he said we must
wait till they chopped a white man. He advised
me if ever I felt like it not to commit a—a barren
felo de se, but to let the Sheshaheli do it. Then
he could report, and then we could mop 'em
up!'

'Most immoral! That's how we got——'
Stalky quoted the name of a province won by just
such a sacrifice.

'Yes, but the beasts dominated one end of my cotton-belt like anything. They chivied me out of it when I went to take soil for analysis—me and Imam Din.'

'Sahib! Is there a need?' The voice came out of the darkness, and the eyes shone over Adam's shoulder ere it ceased.

'None. The name was taken in talk.' Adam abolished him with a turn of the finger. 'I couldn't make a *casus belli* of it just then, because my Chief had taken all the troops to hammer a gang of slave Kings up north. Did you ever hear of our war against Ibn Makarrah? He precious nearly lost us the Protectorate at one time, though he's an ally of ours now.'

'Wasn't he rather a pernicious brute, even as they go?' said Stalky. 'Wade told me about him last year.'

'Well, his nickname all through the country was "The Merciful," and he didn't get *that* for nothing. None of our people ever breathed his proper name. They said "He" or "That One," and they didn't say it aloud, either. He fought us for eight months.'

'I remember. There was a paragraph about it in one of the papers,' I said.

'We broke him, though. No—the slavers don't come our way, because our men have the reputation of dying too much, the first month after they're captured. That knocks down profits, you see.'

'What about your charming friends, the Sheshaheli?' said The Infant.

' There's no market for Sheshaheli.   People
would as soon buy crocodiles.   I believe, before
we annexed the country, Ibn Makarrah dropped
down on 'em once—to train his young men—and
simply hewed 'em in pieces.   The bulk of my
people are agriculturists—just the right stamp for
cotton-growers. . . .   What's Mother playing?—
" *Once in royal*—"? '

The organ that had been crooning as happily
as a woman over her babe restored, steadied to a
tune.

' Magnificent!   Oh, magnificent! ' said The
Infant loyally.   I had never heard him sing but
once, and then, though it was early in the tolerant
morning, his Mess had rolled him into a lotus
pond.

' How did you get your cannibals to work for
you? ' asked Strickland.

' They got converted to civilisation after my
Chief smashed Ibn Makarrah—just at the time
I wanted 'em.   You see, my Chief had promised
me in writing that if I could scrape up a surplus
he would not bag it for his roads this time, but I
might have it for my cotton-play.   I only needed
two hundred pounds.   Our revenues didn't run
to it.'

' What is your revenue? ' Stalky asked in the
vernacular.

' With hut-tax, traders', game and mining
licences, not more than fourteen thousand rupees ;
every penny of it ear-marked months ahead.'
Adam sighed.

' Also there is a fine for dogs straying in the

Sahib's camp. Last year it exceeded three rupees,'
Imam Din said quietly.

' Well, I thought that was fair. They howled
so. We were rather strict on fines. I worked up
my native clerk—Bulaki Ram—to a ferocious
pitch of enthusiasm. He used to calculate the
profits of our cotton-scheme to three points of
decimals, after office. I tell you I envied your
magistrates here hauling money out of motorists
every week ! I had managed to make our
ordinary revenue and expenditure just about meet,
and I was crazy to get the odd two hundred
pounds for my cotton. That sort of thing grows
on a chap when he's alone—and talks aloud ! '

' Hul-lo ! Have you been there already ? ' the
father said, and Adam nodded.

' Yes. Used to spout what I could remember
of *Marmion* to a tree, sir. Well, *then* my luck
turned. One evening an English-speaking nigger
came in towing a corpse by the feet. (You get
used to little things like that.) He said he'd
found it, and please would I identify, because if it
was one of Ibn Makarrah's men there might be
a reward. It was an old Mohammedan, with a
strong dash of Arab—a small-boned, bald-headed
chap, and I was just wondering how it had kept
so well in our climate when it sneezed. You ought
to have seen the nigger ! He fetched a howl and
bolted like—like the dog in *Tom Sawyer*, when he
sat on the what's-its-name beetle. He yelped as
he ran, and the corpse went on sneezing. I could
see it had been *sarkied*. (That's a sort of gum-
poison, pater, which attacks the nerve-centres.

Our Chief Medical Officer is writing a mono-
graph about it.) So Imam Din and I emptied
out the corpse one-time, with my shaving soap
and trade gunpowder, and hot water.

'I'd seen a case of *sarkie* before; so when the
skin peeled off his feet, and he stopped sneezing,
I knew he'd live. He *was* bad, though. Lay like
a log for a week while Imam Din and I massaged
the paralysis out of him. Then he told us he was
a Hajji—had been three times to Mecca—come
in from French Africa, and that he'd met the
nigger by the wayside—just like a case of *thuggee*,
in India—and the nigger had poisoned him.
That seemed reasonable enough by what I knew
of Coast niggers.'

'You believed him?' said his father keenly.

'There was no reason I shouldn't. The nigger
never came back, and the old man stayed with me
for two months,' Adam returned. 'You know
what the best type of a Mohammedan gentleman
can be, pater? He was that.'

'None finer, none finer,' was the answer.

'Except a Sikh,' Stalky grunted.

'He'd been to Bombay; he knew French
Africa inside out; he could quote poetry and the
Koran all day long. He played chess—you don't
know what that meant to me—like a master. We
used to talk about the regeneration of Turkey
and the Sheikh-ul-Islam between moves. Oh,
everything under the sun we talked about! He
was awfully open-minded. He believed in slavery,
of course, but he quite saw that it would have to
die out. That's why he agreed with me about

developing the resources of the district—by cotton-growing, you know.'

'You talked that too?' said Strickland.

'Rather. We discussed it for hours. You don't know what it meant to me. A wonderful man. Imam Din, was not our Hajji marvellous?'

'Most marvellous! It was all through the Hajji that we found the money for our cotton-play.' Imam Din had moved, I fancy, behind Strickland's chair.

'Yes. It must have been dead against his convictions too. He brought me news when I was down with fever at Dupé that one of Ibn Makarrah's men was parading through my District with a bunch of slaves—in the Fork!'[1]

'What's the matter with the Fork, that you can't abide it?' said Stalky. Adam's voice had risen at the last word.

'Local etiquette, sir,' he replied, too earnest to notice Stalky's atrocious pun. 'If a slaver runs slaves through British territory he ought to pretend that they're his servants. Hawkin' 'em about in the Fork—the forked stick that you put round their necks, you know—is insolence—same as not backing your top-sails in the old days. Besides, it unsettles the District.'

'I thought you said slavers didn't come your way,' I put in.

'They don't. But my Chief was smoking 'em out of the North all that season, and they were bolting into French territory any road they could find. My orders were to take no notice so long

[1] *Kanta* in Hindi.

as they circulated, but open slave-dealing in—the
—Fork was too much. I couldn't go myself, so
I told a couple of our Makalali police and Imam
Din to make talk with the gentlemen one-time. It
was rather risky, and it might have been expensive,
but it turned up trumps. They were back in a
few days with the slaver (he didn't show fight)
and a whole crowd of witnesses, and we tried him
in my bedroom, and fined him properly. Just
to show you how demoralised the brute must have
been (Arabs often go dotty after a defeat), he'd
snapped up four or five utterly useless Sheshaheli,
and was offering 'em to all and sundry along the
road. Why, he offered 'em to you, didn't he,
Imam Din?'

' I was witness that he offered man-eaters for
sale,' said Imam Din.

' Luckily for my cotton-scheme, that landed
him both ways. You see, he had slaved *and*
exposed slaves for sale in British territory. That
meant the double fine if I could get it out of him.'

' What was his defence?' said Strickland, late
of the Punjab Police.

' As far as I remember—but I had a tempera-
ture of 104 degrees at the time—he'd mistaken
the meridians of longitude. Thought he was in
French territory. Said he'd never do it again, if
we'd let him off with a fine. I could have shaken
hands with the brute for that. He paid up cash
like a motorist and went off one-time.'

' Did you see him?'

' Ye-es. Didn't I, Imam Din?'

' Assuredly the Sahib both saw and spoke to

the slaver. And the Sahib also made a speech to
the man-eaters when he freed them, and they
swore to supply him with labour for all his cotton-
play. The Sahib leaned on his own servant's
shoulder the while.'

'I remember something of that. I remember
Bulaki Ram giving me the papers to sign, and I
distinctly remember him locking up the money
in the safe—two hundred and ten beautiful English sovereigns. You don't know what that meant
to me! I believe it cured my fever; and as soon
as I could I staggered off with the Hajji to inter-
view the Sheshaheli about labour. *Then* I found
out why they had been so keen to work! It
wasn't gratitude. Their big village had been hit
by lightning and burned out a week or two
before, and they lay flat in rows around me asking
me for a job. I gave it 'em.'

'And so you were very happy?' His mother
had stolen up behind us. 'You liked your cotton,
dear?' She tidied the lump away.

'By Jove, I was happy,' Adam yawned.
'Now if any one'—he looked at The Infant—
'cares to put a little money into the scheme, it'll
be the making of my District. I can't give you
figures, sir, but I assure——'

'You'll take your arsenic, and Imam Din'll
take you up to bed, and I'll come and tuck you
in.'

Agnes leaned forward, her rounded elbows on
his shoulders, hands joined across his dark hair,
and—'Isn't he a darling?' she said to us, with
just the same heart-rending lift of the left eye-

brow and the same break of her voice as sent
Strickland mad among the horses in the year '84.
We were quiet when they were gone. We waited
till Imam Din returned to us from above and
coughed at the door, as only dark-hearted Asia
can.

'Now,' said Strickland, 'tell us what truly
befell, son of my servant.'

'All befell as our Sahib has said. Only—only
there was an arrangement—a little arrangement
on account of his cotton-play.'

'Tell! Sit! I *beg* your pardon, Infant,' said
Strickland.

But The Infant had already made the sign, and
we heard Imam Din hunker down on the floor.
One gets little out of the East at attention.

'When the fever came on our Sahib in our
roofed house at Dupé,' he began, 'the Hajji
listened intently to his talk. He expected the
names of women; though I had already told him
that Our virtue was beyond belief or compare, and
that Our sole desire was this cotton-play. Being
at last convinced, the Hajji breathed on our Sahib's
forehead, to sink into his brain, news concerning
a slave-dealer in his District who had made a mock
of the law. Sahib,'—Imam Din turned to Strickland—' our Sahib answered to those false words
as a horse of blood answers to the spur. He sat
up. He issued orders for the apprehension of
the slave-dealer. Then he fell back. Then we
left him.'

'Alone—servant of my son, and son of my
servant?' said his father.

' There was an old woman which belonged to the Hajji. She had come in with the Hajji's money-belt. The Hajji told her that if our Sahib died, she would die with him. And truly our Sahib had given me orders to depart.'

' Being mad with fever—eh? '

' What could we do, Sahib? This cotton-play was his heart's desire. He talked of it in his fever. Therefore it was his heart's desire that the Hajji went to fetch. Doubtless the Hajji could have given him money enough out of hand for ten cotton-plays, but in this respect also our Sahib's virtue was beyond belief or compare. Great Ones do not exchange moneys. Therefore the Hajji said—and I helped with my counsel—that we must make arrangements to get the money in all respects conformably with the English Law. It was great trouble to us, but—the Law is the Law. And the Hajji showed the old woman the knife by which she would die if our Sahib died. So I accompanied the Hajji.'

' Knowing who he was? ' said Strickland.

' No! Fearing the man. A virtue went out from him overbearing the virtue of lesser persons. The Hajji told Bulaki Ram the clerk to occupy the seat of government at Dupé till our return. Bulaki Ram feared the Hajji, because the Hajji had often gloatingly appraised his skill in figures at five thousand rupees upon any slave-block. The Hajji then said to me: " Come, and we will make the man-eaters play the cotton-game for my delight's delight." The Hajji loved our Sahib with the love of a father for his son, of a saved for his saviour, of a Great One for a Great One. But I said: " We cannot go to that Sheshaheli place without a hundred rifles. We have here five." The Hajji said: " I have untied a knot in my head-handkerchief which will be more to us than a thousand." I saw that he had so loosed it that it lay flagwise on his shoulder. Then I knew that he was a Great One with virtue in him.

' We came to the highlands of the Sheshaheli on the dawn of the second day—about the time of the stirring of the cold wind. The Hajji walked delicately across the open place where their filth is, and scratched upon the gate which was shut. When it opened I saw the man-eaters lying on their cots under the eaves of the huts. They rolled off: they rose up, one behind the other the length of the street; and the fear on their faces was as leaves whitening to a breeze. The Hajji stood in the gate guarding his skirts from defilement. The Hajji said: " I am here once again. Give me six and yoke up." They zealously then pushed to us with poles six, and yoked them with a heavy tree. The Hajji then said: " Fetch fire from the morning hearth, and come to windward." The wind is strong on those headlands at sunrise, so when each had emptied his crock of fire in front of that which was before him, the broadside of the town roared into flame, and all went. The Hajji then said: " At the end of a time there will come here the white man ye once chased for sport. He will demand labour to plant such and such stuff. Ye are that labour, and your spawn after you." They said, lifting their heads a very little from the edge of the ashes: " We are that labour, and our spawn after us." The Hajji said: " What is also my name? " They said: " Thy name is also The Merciful." The Hajji said: " Praise then my mercy "; and while they did this, the Hajji walked away, I following.'

The Infant made some noise in his throat, and reached for more Burgundy.

' About noon one of our six fell dead. Fright —only fright, Sahib! None had—none could— touch him. Since they were in pairs, and the other of the Fork was mad and sang foolishly, we waited for some heathen to do what was needful. There came at last Angari men with goats. The Hajji said: " What do ye see? " They said: " O our Lord, we neither see nor hear." The Hajji said: " But I command ye to see and to hear and to say." They said: " O our Lord, it is to our commanded eyes as though slaves stood in a Fork." The Hajji said: " So testify before the officer who waits you in the town of Dupé." They said: " What shall come to us after? " The Hajji said: " The just reward for the informer. But if ye do *not* testify, then a punishment which shall cause birds to fall from the trees in terror and monkeys to scream for pity." Hearing this, the Angari men hastened to Dupé. The Hajji then said to me: " Are these things sufficient to establish our case, or must I drive in a village full? " I said that three witnesses amply established any case, but as yet, I said, the Hajji had not offered his slaves for sale. It is true, as our Sahib said just now, there is one fine

for catching slaves, and yet another for making to
sell them. And it was the *double* fine that we
needed, Sahib, for our Sahib's cotton-play. We
had fore-arranged all this with Bulaki Ram, who
knows the English Law, and I thought the Hajji
remembered. But he grew angry, and cried out:
" O God, Refuge of the Afflicted, must I, who
am what I am, peddle this dog's meat by the
roadside to gain his delight for my heart's
delight?" None the less, he admitted it was the
English Law, and so he offered me the six—five
—in a small voice, with an averted head. The
Sheshaheli do not smell of sour milk as heathen
should. They smell like leopards, Sahib. This
is because they eat men.'

'Maybe,' said Strickland. 'But where were
thy wits? One witness is not sufficient to establish
the fact of a sale.'

'What could we do, Sahib? There was the
Hajji's reputation to consider. We could not
have called in an heathen witness for such a thing.
And, moreover, the Sahib forgets that the de-
fendant him*self* was making this case. He would
not contest his own evidence. Otherwise I know
the law of evidence well enough.

'So then we went to Dupé, and while Bulaki
Ram waited among the Angari men, I ran to see
our Sahib in bed. His eyes were very bright, and
his mouth was full of upside-down orders, but
the old woman had not loosened her hair for
death. The Hajji said : " Be quick with my trial.
I am not Job!" The Hajji was a learned man.
We made the trial swiftly to a sound of soothing

voices round the bed. Yet—*yet*, because no man can be sure whether a Sahib of that blood sees, or does not see, we made it strictly in the manner of the forms of the English Law. Only the witnesses and the slaves and the prisoner we kept without for his nose's sake.'

'Then he did not see the prisoner?' said Strickland.

' I stood by to shackle up an Angari in case he should demand it, but by God's favour he was too far fevered to ask for one. It is quite true he signed the papers. It is quite true he saw the money put away in the safe—two hundred and ten English pounds—and it is quite true that the gold wrought on him as a strong cure. But as to his seeing the prisoner, and having speech with the man-eaters—the Hajji breathed all that on his forehead to sink into his sick brain. A little, as ye have heard, has remained. . . . Ah, but when the fever broke, and our Sahib called for the fine-book, and the thin little picture-books from Europe with the pictures of ploughs and hoes, and cotton-mills—ah, then he laughed as he used to laugh, Sahib. It was his heart's desire, this cotton-play. The Hajji loved him, as who does not? It was a little, little arrangement, Sahib, of which—*is* it necessary to tell all the world?'

' And when didst thou know who the Hajji was?' said Strickland.

' Not for a certainty till he and our Sahib had returned from their visit to the Sheshaheli country. It is quite true as our Sahib says, the man-eaters lay flat around his feet, and asked for spades to cultivate cotton. That very night, when I was cooking the dinner, the Hajji said to me: " I go to my own place, though God knows whether the Man with the Stone Eyes have left me an ox, a slave, or a woman." I said: " Thou art then *That* One?" The Hajji said: " I am ten thousand rupees reward into thy hand. Shall we make another law case and get more cotton machines for the boy?" I said: " Whose dog am I to do this? May God prolong thy life a thousand years!" The Hajji said: " Who has seen to-morrow? God has given me as it were a son in my old age, and I praise Him. See that the breed is not lost!"

' He walked then from the cooking-place to our Sahib's office-table under the tree, where our Sahib held in his hand a blue envelope of Service newly come in by runner from the North. At this, fearing evil news for the Hajji, I would have restrained him, but he said: " We be both Great Ones. Neither of us will fail." Our Sahib looked up to invite the Hajji to approach before he opened the letter, but the Hajji stood off till our Sahib had well opened and well read the letter. Then the Hajji said: " Is it permitted to say farewell?" Our Sahib stabbed the letter on the file with a deep and joyful breath and cried a welcome. The Hajji said: " I go to my own place," and he loosed from his neck a chained heart of ambergris set in soft gold and held it forth. Our Sahib snatched it swiftly in the closed fist, down-turned, and said: " If thy name be written hereon, it is needless, for a name is

already engraved on my heart." The Hajji said:
" And on mine also is a name engraved; but
there is no name on the amulet." The Hajji
stooped to our Sahib's feet, but our Sahib raised
and embraced him, and the Hajji covered his
mouth with his shoulder-cloth, because it worked,
and so he went away.'

' And what order was in the Service letter? '
Stalky murmured.

' Only an order for our Sahib to write a report
on some new cattle-sickness. But all orders come
in the same make of envelope. We could not tell
what order it might have been.'

' When he opened the letter—my son—made
he no sign? A cough? An oath? ' Strickland
asked.

' None, Sahib. I watched his hands. They
did not shake. Afterwards he wiped his face,
but he was sweating before from the heat.'

' Did he know? Did he know who the Hajji
was? ' said The Infant in English.

' I am a poor man. Who can say what a Sahib
of that get knows or does not know? But the
Hajji is right. The breed should not be lost. It
is not *very* hot for little children in Dupé, and as
regards nurses, my sister's cousin at Jull——'

' H'm! That is the boy's own concern. I
wonder if his Chief ever knew? ' said Strickland.

' Assuredly,' said Imam Din. ' On the night
before our Sahib went down to the sea, the Great
Sahib—the Man with the Stone Eyes—dined
with him in his camp, I being in charge of the
table. They talked a long while and the Great

Sahib said: "What didst thou think of *That*
One?" (*We* do not say Ibn Makarrah yonder.)
Our Sahib said: "Which one?" The Great
Sahib said: "That One which taught thy man-
eaters to grow cotton for thee. He was in thy
District three months to my certain knowledge,
and I looked by every runner that thou wouldst
send me in his head." Our Sahib said: "If his
head had been needed, another man should have
been appointed to govern my District, for he was
my friend." The Great Sahib laughed and said:
"If I had needed a lesser man in thy place, be
sure I would have sent him, as, if I had needed
the head of That One, be sure I would have sent
men to bring it to me. But tell me now, by what
means didst thou twist him to thy use and our
profit in this cotton-play?" Our Sahib said: "By
God, I did not use that man in any fashion whatever. He was my friend." The Great Sahib said:
"*Toh Vau!* [Bosh!] Tell!" Our Sahib shook
his head as he does—as he did when a child—
and they looked at each other like sword-play
men in the ring at a fair. The Great Sahib
dropped his eyes first and he said: "So be it. I
should, perhaps, have answered thus in my youth.
No matter. I have made treaty with That One
as an ally of the State. Some day he shall tell me
the tale." Then I brought in fresh coffee, and
they ceased. But I do not think That One will
tell the Great Sahib more than our Sahib told him.'
    'Wherefore?' I asked.
    'Because they are both Great Ones, and I
have observed in my life that Great Ones employ

words very little between each other in their
dealings; still less when they speak to a third
concerning those dealings. Also they profit by
silence. . . . Now I think that the mother has
come down from the room, and I will go rub his
feet till he sleeps.'

His ears had caught Agnes's step at the stair-
head, and presently she passed us on her way to
the music-room humming the *Magnificat*.

THE NEW KNIGHTHOOD

W H O gives him the Bath ?
  ' I,' said the wet,
  Rank Jungle-sweat,
' I'll give him the Bath ! '

Who'll sing the psalms ?
  ' We,' said the Palms.
  ' Ere the hot wind becalms,
We'll sing the psalms.'

Who lays on the sword ?
  ' I,' said the Sun,
  ' Before he has done,
I'll lay on the sword.'

Who fastens his belt ?
  ' I,' said Short-Rations.
  ' I know all the fashions
Of tightening a belt ! '

Who buckles his spur ?
  ' I,' said his Chief,
  Exacting and brief,
' I'll give him the spur.'

Who'll shake his hand ?
  ' I,' said the Fever,
  ' And I'm no deceiver,
I'll shake his hand.'

Who brings him the wine ?
  ' I,' said Quinine,
  ' It's a habit of mine.
I'll come with his wine.'

Who'll put him to proof ?
  ' I,' said All Earth,
  ' Whatever he's worth,
I'll put to the proof.'

Who'll choose him for Knight ?
  ' I,' said his Mother,
  ' Before any other,
My very own knight ! '

And after this fashion, adventure to seek,
Was Sir Galahad made—as it might be last week !

The Puzzler

The Puzzler

I HAD not seen Penfentenyou since the Middle 'Nineties, when he was Minister of Ways and Woodsides in De Thouar's first Administration. Last summer, though he nominally held the same portfolio, he was his Colony's Premier in all but name, and the idol of his own Province, which is two and a half times the size of England. Politically, his creed was his growing country; and he came over to England to develop a Great Idea in her behalf.

Believing that he had put it in train, I made haste to welcome him to my house for a week.

That he was chased to my door by his own Agent-General in a motor; that they turned my study into a Cabinet Meeting which I was not invited to attend; that the local telegraph all but broke down beneath the strain of hundred-word coded cables; and that I practically broke into the house of a stranger to get him telephonic facilities on a Sunday, are things I overlook. What I objected to was his ingratitude, while I thus tore up England to help him. So I said: 'Why on earth didn't you see your Opposite Number in Town instead of bringing your office work here?'

' Eh? Who? ' said he, looking up from his fourth cable since lunch.

' See the English Minister for Ways and Woodsides.'

' I saw him,' said Penfentenyou, without enthusiasm.

It seemed that he had called twice on the gentleman, but without an appointment—(' I thought if I wasn't big enough, my business was ')—and each time had found him engaged. A third party intervening, suggested that a meeting might be arranged if due notice were given.

' Then,' said Penfentenyou, ' I called at the office at ten o'clock.'

' But they'd be in bed,' I cried.

' One of the babies was awake. He told me that—that " my sort of questions " '—he slapped the pile of cables—' were only taken between 11 and 2 P.M. So I waited.'

' And when you got to business? ' I asked.

He made a gesture of despair. ' It was like talking to children. They'd never heard of it.'

' And your Opposite Number? '

Penfentenyou described him.

' Hush! You mustn't talk like that! ' I shuddered. ' He's one of the best of good fellows. You should meet him socially.'

' I've done that too,' he said. ' Have you? '

' Heaven forbid! ' I cried. ' But that's the proper thing to say.'

' Oh, he said all the proper things. Only I thought as this was England that they'd more or less have the hang of all the—general hang-together of my Idea. But I had to explain it from the beginning.'

' Ah! They'd probably mislaid the papers,' I said, and I told him the story of a three-million-pound insurrection caused by an Under-Secretary sitting upon a mass of green-labelled correspondence instead of reading it.

' I wonder it doesn't happen every week,' he answered. ' D'you mind my having the Agent-General to dinner again to-night? I'll wire, and he can motor down.'

.   .   .   .

The Agent-General arrived two hours later—a patient and expostulating person, visibly torn between the pulling Devil of a rampant Colony and the placid Baker of a largely uninterested England. But with Penfentenyou behind him he had worked; for he told us that Lord Lundie— the Law Lord—was the final authority on the legal and constitutional aspects of the Great Idea, and to him it must be referred.

' Good Heavens alive!' thundered Penfentenyou. ' I told you to get *that* settled last Christmas.'

' It was the middle of the house-party season,' said the Agent-General mildly. ' Lord Lundie's at Credence Green now—he spends his holidays there. It's only forty miles off.'

' Shan't I disturb his Holiness?' said Penfentenyou heavily. ' Perhaps " my sort of questions," ' he snorted, ' mayn't be discussed except at midnight.'

' Oh, don't be a child!' I said.

' What this country needs,' said Penfentenyou,
' is '—and for ten minutes he trumpeted re-
bellion.

' What *you* need is to pay for your own pro-
tection,' I cut in when he drew breath, and I
showed him a yellowish paper, supplied gratis by
Government, which is called Schedule D.   To
my merciless delight he had never seen the thing
before, and I completed my victory over him and
all the Colonies with a Brassey's *Naval Annual*
and a *Statesman's Year-Book*.

The Agent-General interposed with agent-
generalities (but they were merely provocateurs)
about Ties of Sentiment.

' They   be   blowed!'   said   Penfentenyou.
' What's the good of sentiment towards a Kinder-
garten?'

' Quite so.   Ties of common funk are the
things that bind us together; and the sooner you
new nations realise it the better.   What you need
is an annual invasion.   Then you'd grow up.'

' Thank you!   Thank you!' said the Agent-
General.   ' That's what I am always trying to tell
my people.'

' But, my dear fool,'—Penfentenyou almost
wept—' do you pretend that these banana-
fingered amateurs at home *are* grown up?'

' You poor, serious, pagan man,' I retorted,
' if you take 'em *that* way, you'll wreck your
Great Idea.'

' Will you take him to Lord Lundie's to-
morrow?' said the Agent-General promptly.

' I suppose I must,' I said, ' if you won't.'

'Not me! I'm going home,' said the Agent-General, and departed. (I am glad that I am no Colony's Agent-General.)

. . . . .

Penfentenyou continued to argue about naval contributions till 1.15 A.M. though I was victor from the first.

At ten o'clock I got him and his correspondence into the motor, and he had the decency to ask whether he had been unpolished over-night. I replied that I waited an apology. This he made excuse for renewed arguments, and used wayside shows as illustrations of the decadence of England.

For example, we burst a tyre within a mile of Credence Green, and, to save time, walked into the beautifully-kept little village. His eye was caught by a building of pale-blue tin, stencilled 'Calvinist Chapel,' before whose shuttered windows an Italian organ-grinder with a petticoated monkey was playing 'Dolly Gray.'

'Yes. That's it!' snapped the egoist. 'That's a parable of the general situation in England. And look at those brutes!' A huge household-removals van was halted at a public-house. The men in charge were drinking beer from blue-and-white mugs. It seemed to me a pretty sight, but Penfentenyou said it represented Our National Attitude.

Lord Lundie's summer resting-place we learned was a farm, a little out of the village, up a hill round which curled a high-hedged road. Only an initiated few spend their holidays at Credence Green, and they have trained the house-

holders to keep the place select. Penfentenyou
made a grievance of this as we walked up the lane,
followed at a distance by the organ-grinder.

' Suppose he is having a house-party,' he said.
' Anything's possible in this insane land.'

Just at that minute we found ourselves opposite
an empty villa. Its roof was of black slate, with
bright unweathered ridge-tiling ; its walls were of
blood-coloured brick, cornered and banded with
vermiculated stucco work, and there was cobalt,
magenta, and purest apple-green window-glass on
either side of the front door. The whole was
fenced from the road by a low, brick-pillared,
flint wall, topped with a cast-iron Gothic rail,
picked out in blue and gold.

Tight beds of geranium, calceolaria, and
lobelia speckled the grass-plat, from whose centre
rose one of the finest araucarias (its other name by
the way is ' monkey-puzzler ') that it has ever
been my lot to see. It must have been full thirty
feet high, and its foliage exquisitely answered the
iron railings. Such bijou *ne plus ultras* replete
with all the amenities do not, as I pointed out
to Penfentenyou, transpire outside of England.

A hedge, swinging sharp right, flanked the
garden, and above it on a slope of daisy-dotted
meadows we could see Lord Lundie's tiled and
half-timbered summer farm-house. Of a sudden
we heard voices behind the tree—the fine full
tones of the unembarrassed English, speaking to
their equals—that tore through the hedge like
sleet through rafters.

' That it is not called " monkey-puzzler " for

nothing, I willingly concede '—this was a rich
and rolling note—' but on the other hand——'

' I submit, me lud, that the name implies that
it might, could, would, or should be ascended by
a monkey, and *not* that the ascent is a physical
impossibility. I believe one of our South American spider monkeys wouldn't hesitate. . . . By
Jove, it might be worth trying, if——'

This was a crisper voice than the first. A
third, higher-pitched, and full of pleasant affec-
tations, broke in.

' Oh, practical men, there is no ape here.
Why do you waste one of God's own days on
unprofitable discussion ? Give me a match ! '

' I've a good mind to make you demonstrate
in your own person. Come on, Bubbles ! We'll
make Jimmy climb ! '

There was a sound of scuffling, broken by
squeaks from Jimmy of the high voice. I turned
back and drew Penfentenyou into the side of the
flanking hedge. I remembered to have read in a
society paper that Lord Lundie's lesser name was
' Bubbles.'

' What are they doing ? ' Penfentenyou said
sharply. ' Drunk ? '

' Just playing ! Superabundant vitality of the
Race, you know. We'll watch 'em,' I answered.
The noise ceased.

' My deliverer ! ' Jimmy gasped. ' The ram
caught in the thicket, and—I'm the only one
who can talk Neapolitan ! Leggo my collar ! '
He cried aloud in a foreign tongue, and was
answered from the gate.

' It's the Calvinistic organ-grinder,' I whispered. I had already found a practicable break at the bottom of the hedge. ' They're going to try to make the monkey climb, I believe.'

' Here—let me look ! ' Penfentenyou flung himself down, and rooted till he too broke a peephole. We lay side by side commanding the entire garden at ten yards' range.

' You know 'em ? ' said Penfentenyou, as I made some noise or other.

' By sight only. The big fellow in flannels is Lord Lundie ; the light-built one with the yellow beard painted his picture at the last Academy. He's a swell R.A., James Loman.'

' And the brown chap with the hands ? '

' Tomling, Sir Christopher Tomling, the South American engineer who built the——'

' San Juan Viaduct. I know,' said Penfentenyou. ' We ought to have had him with *us.* . . . Do you think a monkey would climb the tree ? '

The organ-grinder at the gate fenced his beast with one arm as Jimmy talked.

' Don't show off your futile accomplishments,' said Lord Lundie. ' Tell him it's an experiment. Interest him ! '

' Shut up, Bubbles. You aren't in court,' Jimmy replied. ' This needs delicacy. Giuseppe says——'

' Interest the monkey,' the brown engineer interrupted. ' He won't climb for love. Cut up to the house and get some biscuits, Bubbles— sugar ones—and an orange or two. No need to tell our womenfolk.'

The huge white figure lobbed off at a trot which would not have disgraced a boy of seventeen. I gathered from something Jimmy let fall that the three had been at Harrow together.

'That Tomling has a head on his shoulders,' muttered Penfentenyou. 'Pity we didn't get him for the Colony. But the question is, will the monkey climb?'

'Be quick, Jimmy. Tell the man we'll give him five bob for the loan of the beast. Now run the organ under the tree, and we'll dress it when Bubbles comes back,' Sir Christopher cried.

'I've often wondered,' said Penfentenyou, 'whether it *would* puzzle a monkey?' He had forgotten the needs of his Growing Nation, and was earnestly parting the white-thorn stems with his fingers.

.   .   .   .   .

Giuseppe and Jimmy did as they were told, the monkey following them with a wary and malignant eye.

'Here's a discovery,' said Jimmy. 'The singing part of this organ comes off the wheels.' He spoke volubly to the proprietor. 'Oh, it's so as Giuseppe can take it to his room o' nights. And play it. D'you hear that? The organ-grinder, after his day's crime, plays his accursed machine for love. For love, Chris! And Michael Angelo was one of 'em!'

'Don't jaw! Tell him to take the beast's petticoat off,' said Sir Christopher Tomling.

Lord Lundie returned, very little winded, through a gap higher up the hedge.

' They're all out, thank goodness ! ' he cried, ' but I've raided what I could. *Marrons glacés*, candied fruit, and a bag of oranges.'

' Excellent ! ' said the world-renowned contractor. ' Jimmy, you're the light-weight ; jump up on the organ and impale these things on the leaves as I hand 'em ! '

' I see,' said Jimmy, capering like a springbok. ' Upward and onward, eh ? First, he'll reach out for—how infernal prickly these leaves are !— this biscuit. Next we'll lure him on—(that's about the reach of his arm)—with the *marron glacé*, and then he'll open out this orange. How human ! How like your ignoble career, Bubbles ! '

With care and elaboration they ornamented that tree's lower branches with sugar-topped biscuits, oranges, bits of banana, and *marrons glacés* till it looked a very ape's path to Paradise.

' Unchain the Gyascutis ! ' said Sir Christopher commandingly. Giuseppe placed the monkey atop of the organ, where the beast, misunderstanding, stood on his head.

' He's throwing himself on the mercy of the Court, me lud,' said Jimmy. ' No—now he's interested. Now he's reaching after higher things. What wouldn't I give to have —— here ! ' (he mentioned a name not unhonoured in British Art). ' Ambition plucking apples of Sodom ! ' (the monkey had pricked himself and was swearing). ' Genius hampered by Convention ! Oh, there's a whole bushelful of allegories in it ! '

' Give him time. He's balancing the probabilities,' said Lord Lundie.

The three closed round the monkey, hanging on his every motion with an earnestness almost equal to ours. The great judge's head—seamed and vertical forehead, iron mouth, and pike-like under-jaw, all set on that thick neck rising out of the white flannel collar—was thrown against the puckered green silk of the organ-front as it might have been a cameo of Titus. Jimmy, with raised eyes and parted lips, fingered his grizzled chestnut beard, and I was near enough to note the capable beauty of his hands. Sir Christopher stood a little apart, his arms folded behind his back, one heavy brown boot thrust forward, chin in as curbed, and black eyebrows lowered to shade the keen eyes. Giuseppe's dark face between flashing earrings, a twisted rag of red and yellow silk round his throat, turned from the reaching yearning monkey to the pink-and-white biscuits spiked on the bronzed leafage. And upon them all fell the serious and workmanlike sun of an English summer forenoon.

'*Fils de Saint Louis, montez au ciel!*' said Lord Lundie suddenly in a voice that made me think of Black Caps. I do not know what the monkey thought, because at that instant he leaped off the organ and disappeared.

There was a clash of broken glass behind the tree.

The monkey's face, distorted with passion, appeared at an upper window of the house, and a starred hole in the stained-glass window to the left of the front door showed the first steps of his upward path.

'We've got to catch him,' cried Sir Christopher. 'Come along!'

They pushed at the door, which was unlocked.

'Yes. But consider the ethics of the case,' said Jimmy. 'Isn't this burglary or something, Bubbles?'

'Settle that when he's caught,' said Sir Christopher. 'We're responsible for the beast.'

A furious clanging of bells broke out of the empty house, followed by muffled gurglings and trumpetings.

'What the deuce is that?' I asked, half aloud.

'The plumbing, of course,' said Penfentenyou. 'What a pity! I believe he'd have climbed if Lord Lundie hadn't put him off!'

'Wait a moment, Chris,' said Jimmy the interpreter. 'Giuseppe says he may answer to the music of his infancy. Giuseppe therefore will go in with the organ. Orpheus with his lute, you know. *Avanti*, Orpheus! There's no Neapolitan for bathroom, but I fancy your friend is there.'

'I'm not going into another man's house with a hurdy-gurdy,' said Lord Lundie, recoiling, as Giuseppe unshipped the working mechanism of the organ (it developed a hang-down leg) from its wheels, slipped a strap round his shoulders, and gave the handle a twist.

'Don't be a cad, Bubbles,' was Jimmy's answer. 'You couldn't leave us now if you were on the Woolsack. Play, Orpheus! The Cadi accompanies.'

.   .   .   .   .

With a whoop, a buzz, and a crash, the organ

sprang to life under the hand of Giuseppe, and the procession passed through the grained-to-imitate-walnut front door. A moment later we saw the monkey ramping on the roof.

'He'll be all over the township in a minute if we don't head him,' said Penfentenyou, leaping to his feet, and crashing into the garden. We headed him with pebbles till he retired through a window to the tuneful reminder that he had left a lot of little things behind him. As we passed the front door it swung open, and showed Jimmy the artist sitting at the bottom of a newly-cleaned staircase. He waggled his hands at us, and when we entered we saw that the man was stricken speechless. His eyes grew red—red like a ferret's—and what little breath he had whistled shrilly. At first we thought it was a fit, and then we saw that it was mirth—the inopportune mirth of the Artistic Temperament.

The house palpitated to an infamous melody punctuated by the stump of the barrel-organ's one leg, as Giuseppe, above, moved from room to room after his rebel slave. Now and again a floor shook a little under the combined rushes of Lord Lundie and Sir Christopher Tomling, who gave many and contradictory orders. But when they could they cursed Jimmy with splendid thoroughness.

'Have you anything to do with the house?' panted Jimmy at last. 'Because we're using it just now.' He gulped. 'And I'm—ah—keeping cavè.'

'All right,' said Penfentenyou, and shut the hall door.

'Jimmy, you unspeakable blackguard! Jimmy, you cur! You coward!' (Lord Lundie's voice overbore the flood of melody.) 'Come up here! Giuseppe's saying something we don't understand.'

Jimmy listened and interpreted between hiccups.

'He says you'd better play the organ, Bubbles, and let him do the stalking. The monkey knows him.'

'By Jove, he's quite right,' said Sir Christopher from the landing. 'Take it, Bubbles, at once.'

'My God!' said Lord Lundie in horror.

The chase reverberated over our heads, from the attics to the first floor and back again. Bodies and voices met in collision and argument, and once or twice the organ hit walls and doors. Then it broke forth in a new manner.

'*He*'s playing it,' said Jimmy. 'I know his acute Justinian ear. Are you fond of music?'

'I think Lord Lundie plays very well for a beginner,' I ventured.

'Ah! That's the trained legal intellect. Like mastering a brief. I haven't got it.' He wiped his eyes and shook.

'Hi!' said Penfentenyou, looking through the stained-glass window down the garden. 'What's that!'

.   .   .   .   .

A household-removals van, in charge of four men, had halted at the gate. A husband and his wife—householders beyond question—quavered irresolutely up the path. He looked tired. She was certainly cross. In all this haphazard world the last couple to understand a scientific experiment.

I laid hands on Jimmy—the clamour above drowning speech—and, with Penfentenyou's aid, propped him like an umbrella against the window, that he should see.

He saw, nodded, fell as an umbrella can fall, and, kneeling, beat his forehead on the shut door. Penfentenyou slid the bolt.

The furniture men reinforced the two figures on the path, and advanced, spreading generously.

'Hadn't we better warn them upstairs?' I suggested.

'No. I'll die first!' said Jimmy. 'I'm pretty near it now. Besides, they called me names.'

I turned from the Artist to the Administrator.

'*Ceteris paribus*, I think we'd better be going,' said Penfentenyou, dealer in crises.

'Ta—take me with you,' said Jimmy. 'I've no reputation to lose, but I'd like to watch 'em from—er—outside the picture.'

'There's always a *modus vivendi*,' Penfentenyou murmured, and tiptoed along the hall to a back door, which he opened quite silently. We passed into a tangle of gooseberry bushes where, at his statesman-like example, we crawled on all fours, and regained the hedge.

Here we lay up, secure in our alibi.

'But your firm,'—the woman was wailing to the furniture-removals men—'your firm *promised* me everything should be in yesterday. And it's to-day! You should have been here yesterday!'

' The last tenants ain't out yet, lydy,' said one
of them.

Lord Lundie was rapidly improving in tech-
nique, though organ-grinding, unlike the Law, is
more of a calling than a trade, and he hung
occasionally on a dead centre. Giuseppe, I think,
was singing, but I could not understand the drift
of Sir Christopher's remarks. They were Spanish.

The woman said something we did not catch.

' You might 'ave sub-let it,' the man insisted.
' Or your gentleman 'ere might.'

' But I didn't. Send for the Police at once.'

' I wouldn't do that, lydy. They're only fruit-
pickers on a beano. They aren't particular where
they sleep.'

' D'you mean they've been sleeping *there*? I
only had it cleaned last week. Get them out.'

' Oh, if you say so, we'll 'ave 'em out of it in
two twos. Alf, fetch me the spare swingle-bar.'

' Don't! You'll knock the paint off the door.
Get them out ! '

' What the 'ell else am I trying to do for you,
lydy?' the man answered with pathos; but the
woman wheeled on her mate.

' Edward! They're all drunk here, and they're
all mad there. Do something ! ' she said.

Edward took one short step forward, and
sighed ' Hullo ! ' in the direction of the turbulent
house. The woman walked up and down, the
very figure of Domestic Tragedy. The furniture
men swayed a little on their heels, and——

' Got him ! ' The shout rang through all the
windows at once. It was followed by a blood-

hound-like bay from Sir Christopher, a maniacal prestissimo on the organ, and loud cries for Jimmy. But Jimmy, at my side, rolled his congested eyeballs, owl-wise.

' I never knew them,' he said. ' I'm an orphan.'

. . . . .

The front door opened, and the three came forth to short-lived triumph. I had never before seen a Law Lord dressed as for tennis, with a stump-leg barrel-organ strapped to his shoulder. But it is a shy bird in this plumage. Lord Lundie strove to disembarrass himself of his accoutrements much as an ill-trained Punch and Judy dog tries to escape backwards through his frilled collar. Sir Christopher, covered with lime-wash, cherished a bleeding thumb, and the almost crazy monkey tore at Giuseppe's hair.

The men on both sides reeled, but the woman stood her ground. ' Idiots ! ' she said, and once more, ' Idiots ! '

I could have gladdened a few convicts of my acquaintance with a photograph of Lord Lundie at that instant.

' Madam,' he began, wonderfully preserving the roll in his voice, ' it was a monkey.'

Sir Christopher sucked his thumb and nodded.

' Take it away and go,' she replied. ' Go away ! '

I would have gone, and gladly, on this permission, but these still strong men must ever be justifying themselves. Lord Lundie turned to the husband, who for the first time spoke.

P

'I have rented this house. I am moving in,' he said.

'We ought to have been in yesterday,' the woman interrupted.

'Yes. We ought to have been in yesterday. Have you slept there overnight?' said the man peevishly.

'No, I assure you we haven't,' said Lord Lundie.

'Then go away. Go quite away,' cried the woman.

They went—in single file down the path. They went silently, restrapping the organ on its wheels, and rechaining the monkey to the organ.

'Damn it all!' said Penfentenyou. 'They *do* face the music, and they do stick by each other—in private life!'

'Ties of Common Funk,' I answered. Giuseppe ran to the gate and fled back to the possible world. Lord Lundie and Sir Christopher, constrained by tradition, paced slowly.

Then it came to pass that the woman, who walked behind them, lifted up her eyes, and beheld the tree which they had dressed.

'Stop!' she called; and they stopped. 'Who did that?'

There was no answer. The Eternal Bad Boy in every man hung its head before the Eternal Mother in every woman.

'Who put those disgusting things there?' she repeated.

Suddenly Penfentenyou, Premier of his Colony in all but name, left Jimmy and me, and appeared at the gate. (If he is not turned out of office, that is how he will appear on the Day of Armageddon.)

'Well done you!' he cried zealously, and doffed his hat to the woman. 'Have you any children, madam?' he demanded.

'Yes, two. They should have been here to-day. The firm promised——'

'Then we're not a minute too soon. That monkey—escaped. It was a very dangerous beast. Might have frightened your children into fits. All the organ-grinder's fault! A most lucky thing these gentlemen caught it when they did. I hope you aren't badly mauled, Sir Christopher?' Shaken as I was (I wanted to get away and laugh), I could not but admire the scoundrel's consummate tact in leading his second highest trump. An ass would have introduced Lord Lundie and they would not have believed him.

It took the trick. The couple smiled, and gave respectful thanks for their deliverance by such hands from such perils.

'Not in the least,' said Lord Lundie. 'Anybody—any father—would have done as much, and—pray don't apologise—your mistake was quite natural.' A furniture man sniggered here, and Lord Lundie rolled an Eye of Doom on their ranks. 'By the way, if you have trouble with these persons—they seem to have taken as much as is good for them—please let me know. Er—*Good* morning!'

They turned into the lane.

'Heavens!' said Jimmy, brushing himself

down. ' Who's that real man with the real
head?' and we hurried after them, for they were
running unsteadily, squeaking like rabbits as they
ran. We overtook them in a little nut wood half
a mile up the road, where they had turned aside,
and were rolling. So we rolled with them, and
ceased not till we had arrived at the extremity of
exhaustion.

' You—you saw it all, then?' said Lord
Lundie, rebuttoning his nineteen-inch collar.

' I saw it was a vital question from the first,'
responded Penfentenyou, and blew his nose.

' It was. By the way, d'you mind telling me
your name?'

Summa. Penfentenyou's Great Idea has gone
through, a little chipped at the edges, but in fine
and far-reaching shape. His Opposite Number
worked at it like a mule—a bewildered mule,
beaten from behind, coaxed from in front, and
propped on either soft side by Lord Lundie of
the compressed mouth and the searing tongue.

Sir Christopher Tomling has been ravished
from the Argentine, where, after all, he was but
preparing trade-routes for hostile peoples, and
now adorns the forefront of Penfentenyou's
Advisory Board. This was an unforeseen extra,
as was Jimmy's gratis full-length (it will be in
this year's Academy) of Penfentenyou, who has
returned to his own place.

Now and again, from afar off, between the
slam and bump of his shifting scenery, the glare
of his manipulated limelight, and the controlled

rolling of his thunder-drums, I catch his voice, lifted in encouragement and advice to his fellow-countrymen. He is quite sound on Ties of Sentiment, and—alone of Colonial Statesmen—ventures to talk of the Ties of Common Funk.

Herein I have my reward.

THE PUZZLER

THE Celt in all his variants from Builth to Ballyhoo,
His mental processes are plain—one knows what he will do
And can logically predicate his finish by his start :
But the English—ah, the English !—they are quite a race apart.

Their psychology is bovine, their outlook crude and raw ;
They abandon vital matters to be tickled with a straw ;
But the straw that they were tickled with—the chaff that they
 were fed with—
They convert into a weaver's beam to break their foemen's head
 with.

For undemocratic reasons and for motives not of State,
They arrive at their conclusions—largely inarticulate.
Being void of self-expression they confide their views to none ;
But sometimes, in a smoking-room, one learns why things were
 done.

Yes, sometimes, in a smoking-room, through clouds of ' Ers '
 and ' Ums,'
Obliquely and by inference, illumination comes,
On some step that they have taken, on some action they approve—
Embellished with the argot of the Upper Fourth Remove.

In telegraphic sentences, half nodded to their friends,
They hint a matter's inwardness—and there the matter ends.
And while the Celt is talking from Valencia to Kirkwall,
The English—ah, the English !—don't say anything at all !

Little   Foxes

Little Foxes

A fox came out of his earth on the banks of the Great River Gihon, which waters Ethiopia. He saw a white man riding through the dry dhurra-stalks, and, that his destiny might be fulfilled, barked at him.

The rider drew rein among the villagers round his stirrup.

'What,' said he, 'is that?'

'That,' said the Sheikh of the village, 'is a fox, O Excellency Our Governor.'

'It is not, then, a jackal?'

'No jackal, but Abu Hussein, the Father of Cunning.'

'Also,'—the white man spoke half aloud,—' I am Mudir of this Province.'

'It is true,' they cried. 'Ya, Saart el Mudir' [O Excellency Our Governor].

The Great River Gihon, well used to the moods of kings, slid between his mile-wide banks toward the sea, while the Governor praised God in a loud and searching cry never before heard by the River.

When he had lowered his right forefinger from

229

behind his right ear, the villagers talked to him of
their crops—barley, dhurra, millet, onions, and the
like.   The Governor stood up in his stirrups.
North he looked at a strip of green cultivation a
few hundred yards wide which lay like a carpet
between the river and the tawny line of the desert.
Sixty miles that strip stretched before him, and
as many behind.   At every half-mile a groaning
waterwheel lifted the soft water from the river
to the crops by way of a mud-built aqueduct.   A
foot or so wide was the water-channel; five foot
or more high was the bank on which it ran, and
its base was broad in proportion.   Abu Hussein,
misnamed the Father of Cunning, drank from the
river below his earth, and his shadow was long in
the low sun.   He could not understand the loud
cry which the Governor had cried.

The Sheikh of the village spoke of the crops
from which the rulers of all lands draw revenue;
but the Governor's eyes were fixed, between his
horse's ears, on the nearest water-channel.

'Very like a ditch in Ireland,' he murmured,
and smiled, dreaming of a razor-topped bank in
distant Kildare.

Encouraged by that smile, the Sheikh continued.   'When crops fail it is necessary to remit
taxation.   Then it is a good thing, O Excellency
Our Governor, that you should come and see the
crops which have failed, and discover that we have
not lied.'

'Assuredly.'   The Governor shortened his
reins.   The horse cantered on, rose at the embank-
ment of the water-channel, changed leg cleverly

on top, and hopped down in a cloud of golden dust.

Abu Hussein from his earth watched with interest. He had never before seen such things.

'Assuredly,' the Governor repeated, and came back by the way he had gone. 'It is always best to see for one's self.'

An ancient and still bullet-speckled stern-wheel steamer, with a barge lashed to her side, came round the river bend. She whistled to tell the Governor his dinner was ready, and the horse, seeing his fodder piled on the barge, whinnied.

'Moreover,' the Sheikh added, 'in the Days of the Oppression the Emirs and their creatures dispossessed many people of their lands. All up and down the River our people are waiting to return to their lawful fields.'

'Judges have been appointed to settle that matter,' said the Governor. 'They will presently come in steamers and hear the witnesses.'

'Wherefore? Did the Judges kill the Emirs? We would rather be judged by the men who executed God's judgment on the Emirs. We would rather abide by *your* decision, O Excellency Our Governor.'

The Governor nodded. It was a year since he had seen the Emirs stretched close and still round the reddened sheepskin where lay El Mahdi, the Prophet of God. Now there remained no trace of their dominion except the old steamer, once part of a Dervish flotilla, which was his house and office. She sidled into the shore, lowered a plank, and the Governor followed his horse aboard.

Lights burned on her till late, dully reflected in the river that tugged at her mooring-ropes. The Governor read, not for the first time, the administration reports of one John Jorrocks, M.F.H.

' We shall need,' he said suddenly to his Inspector, ' about ten couple. I'll get 'em when I go home. You'll be Whip, Baker? '

The Inspector, who was not yet twenty-five, signified his assent in the usual manner, while Abu Hussein barked at the vast desert moon.

' Ha ! ' said the Governor, coming out in his pyjamas, ' we'll be giving you capivi in another three months, my friend.'

.   .   .   .   .

It was four, as a matter of fact, ere a steamer with a melodious bargeful of hounds anchored at that landing. The Inspector leaped down among them, and the homesick wanderers received him as a brother.

' Everybody fed 'em everything on board ship, but they're real dainty hounds at bottom,' the Governor explained. ' That's Royal you've got hold of—the pick of the bunch—and the bitch that's got hold of you—she's a little excited —is May Queen. Merriman, out of Cottesmore Maudlin, you know.'

' I know. " Grand old betch with the tan eyebrows," ' the Inspector cooed. ' Oh, Ben ! I shall take an interest in life now. Hark to 'em ! Oh, hark ! '

Abu Hussein, under the high bank, went about his night's work. An eddy carried his scent to the barge, and three villages heard the crash of music that followed. Even then Abu Hussein did not know better than to bark in reply.

'Well, what about my Province?' the Governor asked.

'Not so bad,' the Inspector answered, with Royal's head between his knees. 'Of course, all the villages want remission of taxes, but, as far as I can see, the whole country's stinkin' with foxes. Our trouble will be choppin' 'em in cover. I've got a list of the only villages entitled to any remission. What d'you call this flat-sided, blue-mottled beast with the jowl?'

'Beagle-boy. I have my doubts about him. Do you think we can get two days a week?'

'Easy; and as many byes as you please. The Sheikh of this village here tells me that his barley has failed, and he wants a fifty per cent remission.'

'We'll begin with him to-morrow, and look at his crops as we go. Nothing like personal supervision,' said the Governor.

They began at sunrise. The pack flew off the barge in every direction, and, after gambols, dug like terriers at Abu Hussein's many earths. Then they drank themselves pot-bellied on Gihon water while the Governor and the Inspector chastised them with whips. Scorpions were added; for May Queen nosed one, and was removed to the barge lamenting. Mystery (a puppy, alas!) met a snake, and the blue-mottled Beagle-boy (never a dainty hound) ate that which he should have passed by. Only Royal, of the Belvoir tan head and the sad, discerning eyes, made any attempt to uphold the honour of England before the watching village.

'You can't expect everything,' said the Governor after breakfast.

'We got it, though—everything except foxes. Have you seen May Queen's nose?' said the Inspector.

'And Mystery's dead. We'll keep 'em coupled next time till we get well in among the crops. I say, what a babbling body-snatcher that Beagle-boy is! Ought to be drowned!'

'They bury people so dam' casual hereabouts. Give him another chance,' the Inspector pleaded, not knowing that he should live to repent most bitterly.

'Talkin' of chances,' said the Governor, 'this Sheikh lies about his barley bein' a failure. If it's high enough to hide a hound at this time of year, it's all right. And he wants a fifty per cent remission, you said?'

'You didn't go on past the melon patch where I tried to turn Wanderer. It's all burned up from there on to the desert. His other waterwheel has broken down, too,' the Inspector replied.

'Very good. We'll split the difference and allow him twenty-five per cent off. Where'll we meet to-morrow?'

'There's some trouble among the villages down the river about their land-titles. It's good goin' about there too,' the Inspector said.

The next meet, then, was some twenty miles down the river, and the pack were not enlarged till they were fairly among the fields. Abu Hussein

was there in force—four of him. Four delirious
hunts of four minutes each—four hounds per fox
—ended in four earths just above the river. All
the village looked on.

'We forgot about the earths. The banks are
riddled with 'em. This'll defeat us,' said the
Inspector.

'Wait a moment!' The Governor drew forth
a sneezing hound. 'I've just remembered I'm
Governor of these parts.'

'Then turn out a black battalion to stop for
us. We'll need 'em, old man.'

The Governor straightened his back. 'Give
ear, O people!' he cried. 'I make a new
Law!'

The villagers closed in. He called:—

'Henceforward I will give one dollar to the
man on whose land Abu Hussein is found. And
another dollar'—he held up the coin—'to the
man on whose land these dogs shall kill him.
But to the man on whose land Abu Hussein shall
run into a hole such as is this hole, I will give not
dollars, but a most immeasurable beating. Is it
understood?'

'Our Excellency,'—a man stepped forth—
'on my land Abu Hussein was found this morning. Is it not so, brothers?'

None denied. The Governor tossed him over
four dollars without a word.

'On my land they all went into their holes,'
cried another. 'Therefore I must be beaten.'

'Not so. The land is mine, and mine are the
beatings.'

This second speaker thrust forward his shoulders already bared, and the villagers shouted.

'Hullo! Two men anxious to be licked? There must be some swindle about the land,' said the Governor. Then in the local vernacular: 'What are your rights to the beating?'

As a river-reach changes beneath a slant of the sun, that which had been a scattered mob changed to a court of most ancient justice. The hounds tore and sobbed at Abu Hussein's hearthstone, all unnoticed among the legs of the witnesses, and Gihon, also accustomed to laws, purred approval.

'You will not wait till the Judges come up the river to settle the dispute?' said the Governor at last.

'No!' shouted all the village save the man who had first asked to be beaten. 'We will abide by Our Excellency's decision. Let Our Excellency turn out the creatures of the Emirs who stole our land in the Days of the Oppression.'

'And thou sayest?' the Governor turned to the man who had first asked to be beaten.

'I say *I* will wait till the wise Judges come down in the steamer. Then I will bring my many witnesses,' he replied.

'He is rich. He will bring many witnesses,' the village Sheikh muttered.

'No need. Thine own mouth condemns thee!' the Governor cried. 'No man lawfully entitled to his land would wait one hour before entering upon it. Stand aside!' The man fell back, and the village jeered him.

The second claimant stooped quickly beneath the lifted hunting-crop. The village rejoiced.

' O Such an one ; Son of such an one,' said the Governor, prompted by the Sheikh, ' learn, from the day when I send the order, to block up all the holes where Abu Hussein may hide—on—thy—land ! '

The light flicks ended. The man stood up triumphant. By that accolade had the Supreme Government acknowledged his title before all men.

While the village praised the perspicacity of the Governor, a naked, pock-marked child strode forward to the earth, and stood on one leg, unconcerned as a young stork.

' Ha ! ' he said, hands behind his back. ' This should be blocked up with bundles of dhurra stalks—or, better, bundles of thorns.'

' Better thorns,' said the Governor. ' Thick ends innermost.'

The child nodded gravely and squatted on the sand.

' An evil day for thee, Abu Hussein,' he shrilled into the mouth of the earth. ' A day of obstacles to thy flagitious returns in the morning ! '

' Who is it ? ' the Governor asked the Sheikh. ' It thinks.'

' Farag the Fatherless. His people were slain in the Days of the Oppression. The man to whom Our Excellency has awarded the land is, as it were, his maternal uncle.'

' Will it come with me and feed the big dogs ? ' said the Governor.

The other peering children drew back. ' Run ! '
they cried. ' Our Excellency will feed Farag to
the big dogs.'

' I will come,' said Farag. ' And I will never
go.' He threw his arm round Royal's neck, and
the wise beast licked his face.

' Binjamin, by Jove ! ' the Inspector cried.

' No ! ' said the Governor. ' I believe he has
the making of James Pigg ! '

Farag waved his hand to his uncle, and led
Royal on to the barge. The rest of the pack
followed.

.   .   .   .   .

Gihon, that had seen many sports, learned to
know the Hunt barge well. He met her rounding
his bends on grey December dawns to music wild
and lamentable as the almost forgotten throb of
Dervish drums, when, high above Royal's tenor
bell, sharper even than lying Beagle-boy's falsetto
break, Farag chanted deathless war against Abu
Hussein and all his seed. At sunrise the River
would shoulder her carefully into her place, and
listen to the rush and scutter of the pack fleeing
up the gang-plank, and the tramp of the Governor's Arab behind them. They would pass over
the brow into the dewless crops, where Gihon,
low and shrunken, could only guess what they
were about when Abu Hussein flew down the
bank to scratch at a stopped earth, and flew back
into the barley again. As Farag had foretold, it
was evil days for Abu Hussein ere he learned to
take the necessary steps and to get away crisply.
Sometimes Gihon saw the whole procession of the

Hunt silhouetted against the morning blue, bearing him company for many merry miles.   At
every half mile the horses and the donkeys jumped
the water-channels—up, on, change your leg, and
off again—like figures in a zoetrope, till they grew
small along the line of waterwheels.   Then Gihon
waited their rustling return through the crops,
and took them to rest on his bosom at ten o'clock.
While the horses ate, and Farag slept with his
head on Royal's flank, the Governor and his
Inspector worked for the good of the Hunt and
his Province.

After a little time there was no need to beat any
man for neglecting his earths.   The steamer's
destination was telegraphed from waterwheel to
waterwheel, and the villagers stopped out and put
to according.   If an earth were overlooked, it
meant some dispute as to the ownership of the
land, and then and there the Hunt checked and
settled it in this wise: The Governor and the
Inspector side by side, but the latter half a horse's
length to the rear; both bare-shouldered claim-
ants well in front;   the villagers half-mooned
behind them, and Farag with the pack, who quite
understood the performance, sitting down on the
left.   Twenty minutes were enough to settle the
most complicated case, for, as the Governor said
to a real Judge on the steamer, ' One gets at the
truth in a hunting-field a heap quicker than in
your law-courts.'

' But when the evidence is conflicting?' the
Judge suggested.

' Watch the field.   They'll throw tongue fast

enough if you're running a wrong scent. You've never had an appeal from one of my decisions yet.'

The Sheikhs on horseback—the lesser folk on clever donkeys—the children so despised by Farag —soon understood that villages which repaired their waterwheels and channels stood highest in the Governor's favour. He bought their barley for his horses.

'Channels,' he said, 'are necessary that we may all jump them. They are necessary, moreover, for the crops. Let there be many wheels and sound channels—and much good barley.'

'Without money,' replied an aged Sheikh, 'there can be no waterwheels.'

'I will lend the money,' said the Governor.

'At what interest, O Our Excellency?'

'Take you two of May Queen's puppies to bring up in your village in such a manner that they do not eat filth, nor lose their hair, nor catch fever from lying in the sun, but become wise hounds.'

'Like Ray-yal—not like Bigglebai?' (already it was an insult along the River to compare a man to the shifty anthropophagous blue-mottled harrier).

'Certainly, like Ray-yal—not in the least like Bigglebai. *That* shall be the interest on the loan. Let the puppies thrive and the waterwheel be built, and I shall be content,' said the Governor.

'The wheel shall be built, but, O Our Excellency, if by God's favour the pups grow to be well-smellers, not filth-eaters, not unaccustomed to their names, not lawless, who will do them and me justice at the time of judging the young dogs?'

'Hounds, man, hounds! Ha-wands, O Sheikh, we call them in their manhood.'

'The ha-wands when they are judged at the Sha-ho. I have unfriends down the river to whom Our Excellency has also entrusted ha-wands to bring up.'

'Puppies, man! Pah-peaz, we call them, O Sheikh, in their childhood.'

'Pah-peaz. My enemies may judge my pah-peaz unjustly at the Sha-ho. This must be thought of.'

'I see the obstacle. Hear now! If the new waterwheel is built in a month without oppression, thou, O Sheikh, shalt be named one of the judges to judge the pah-peaz at the Sha-ho. Is it understood?'

'Understood. We will build the wheel. I and my seed are responsible for the repayment of the loan. Where are my pah-peaz? If they eat fowls, must they on any account eat the feathers?'

'On no account must they eat the feathers. Farag in the barge will tell thee how they are to live.'

There is no instance of any default on the Governor's personal and unauthorised loans, for which they called him the Father of Waterwheels. But the first puppy-show at the capital needed enormous tact and the presence of a black battalion ostentatiously drilling in the barrack square to prevent trouble after the prize-giving.

But who can chronicle the glories of the Gihon Hunt—or their shames? Who remembers the kill in the market-place, when the Governor bade the assembled Sheikhs and warriors observe how the hounds would instantly devour the body of Abu Hussein; but how, when he had scientifically broken it up, the weary pack turned from it in loathing, and Farag wept because he said the world's face had been blackened? What men who have not yet ridden beyond the sound of any horn recall the midnight run which ended— Beagle-boy leading—among tombs; the hasty whip-off, and the oath, taken above bones, to forget the worry? That desert run, when Abu Hussein forsook the cultivation, and made a six-mile point to earth in a desolate khor—when strange armed riders on camels swooped out of a ravine, and, instead of giving battle, offered to take the tired hounds home on their beasts. Which they did, and vanished.

Above all, who remembers the death of Royal, when a certain Sheikh wept above the body of the stainless hound as it might have been his son's— and that day the Hunt rode no more? The badly kept log-book says little of this, but at the end of their second season (forty-nine brace) appears the dark entry: 'New blood badly wanted. They are beginning to listen to Beagle-boy.'

·   ·   ·   ·   ·

The Inspector attended to the matter when his leave fell due.

'Remember,' said the Governor, 'you must get us the best blood in England—real, dainty hounds—expense no object, but don't trust your own judgment. Present my letters of introduction, and take what they give you.'

The Inspector presented his letters in a society where they make much of horses, more of hounds, and are tolerably civil to men who can ride. They passed him from house to house, mounted him according to his merits, and fed him, after five years of goat chop and Worcester sauce, perhaps a thought too richly.

The seat or castle where he made his great coup does not much matter. Four Masters of Foxhounds were at table, and in a mellow hour the Inspector told them stories of the Gihon Hunt. He ended: 'Ben said I wasn't to trust my own judgment about hounds; but *I* think there ought to be a special tariff for Empire-makers.'

As soon as his hosts could speak, they reassured him on this point.

' And now tell us about your first puppy-show all over again,' said one.

' And about the earth-stoppin'. Was that all Ben's own invention?' said another.

' Wait a moment,' said a large, clean-shaven man—not an M.F.H.—at the end of the table. ' Are your villagers habitually beaten by your Governor when they fail to stop foxes' holes?'

The tone and the phrase were enough, even if, as the Inspector confessed afterwards, the big, blue double-chinned man had not looked so like Beagle-boy. He took him on for the honour of Ethiopia.

' We only hunt twice a week—sometimes three times. I've never known a man chastised more than four times a week—unless there's a bye.'

The large loose-lipped man flung his napkin down, came round the table, cast himself into the chair next the Inspector, and leaned forward earnestly, so that he breathed in the Inspector's face.

' Chastised with what? ' he said.

' With the *kourbash*—on the feet. A *kourbash* is a strip of old hippo-hide with a sort of keel on it, like the cutting edge of a boar's tusk. But we use the rounded side for a first offender.'

' And do any consequences follow this sort of thing? For the victim, I mean—not for you? '

' Ve-ry rarely. Let me be fair. I've never seen a man die under the lash, but gangrene may set up if the *kourbash* has been pickled.'

' Pickled in what? ' All the table was still and interested.

' In copperas, of course. Didn't you know *that*? ' said the Inspector.

' Thank God I didn't.' The large man sputtered visibly.

The Inspector wiped his face and grew bolder.

' You mustn't think we're careless about our earth-stoppers. We've a Hunt fund for hot tar. Tar's a splendid dressing if the toe-nails aren't beaten off. But huntin' as large a country as we do, we mayn't be back at that village for a month, and if the dressings ain't renewed, and gangrene sets in, often as not you find your man pegging about on his stumps. We've a well-known local

name for 'em down the river. We call 'em the
Mudir's Cranes. You see, I persuaded the
Governor to bastinado only on one foot.'

'On one foot? The Mudir's Cranes!' The
large man turned purple to the top of his bald
head. 'Would you mind giving me the local
word for Mudir's Cranes?'

From a too well stocked memory the Inspector
drew one short adhesive word which surprises by
itself even unblushing Ethiopia. He spelt it out,
saw the large man write it down on his cuff and
withdraw. Then the Inspector translated a few
of its significations and implications to the four
Masters of Foxhounds. He left three days later
with eight couple of the best hounds in England
—a free and a friendly and an ample gift from
four packs to the Gihon Hunt. He had honestly
meant to undeceive the large blue-mottled man,
but somehow forgot about it.

The new draft marks a new chapter in the
Hunt's history. From an isolated phenomenon
in a barge it became a permanent institution with
brick-built kennels ashore, and an influence,
social, political, and administrative, coterminous
with the boundaries of the Province. Ben, the
Governor, departed to England, where he kept a
pack of real dainty hounds, but never ceased to
long for the old lawless lot. His successors were
ex-officio Masters of the Gihon Hunt, as all Inspectors were Whips. For one reason, Farag, the
kennel-huntsman, in khaki and puttees, would
obey nothing under the rank of an Excellency,
and the hounds would obey no one but Farag;

for another, the best way of estimating crop returns and revenue was by riding straight to hounds; for a third, though Judges down the river issued signed and sealed land-titles to all lawful owners, yet public opinion along the river never held any such title valid till it had been confirmed, according to precedent, by the Governor's hunting-crop in the hunting-field, above the wilfully neglected earth. True, the ceremony had been cut down to three mere taps on the shoulder, but Governors who tried to evade that much found themselves and their office compassed about with a great cloud of witnesses who took up their time with lawsuits and, worse still, neglected the puppies. The older Sheikhs, indeed, stood out for the immeasurable beatings of the old days— the sharper the punishment, they argued, the surer the title; but here the hand of modern progress was against them, and they contented themselves with telling tales of Ben the first Governor, whom they called the Father of Waterwheels, and of that heroic age when men, horses, and hounds were worth following.

This same Modern Progress which brought dog-biscuit and brass water-taps to the kennels was at work all over the world. Forces, Activities, and Movements sprang into being, agitated themselves, coalesced, and, in one political avalanche, overwhelmed a bewildered, and not in the least intending it, England. The echoes of the New Era were borne into the Province on the wings of inexplicable cables. The Gihon Hunt read speeches and sentiments and policies which amazed them, and they thanked God, prematurely, that their Province was too far off, too hot, and too hard-worked to be reached by those speakers or their policies. But they, with others, underestimated the scope and purpose of the New Era.

One by one the Provinces of the Empire were hauled up and baited, hit and held, lashed under the belly, and forced back on their haunches for the amusement of their new masters in the parish of Westminster. One by one they fell away, sore and angry, to compare stripes with each other at the ends of the uneasy earth. Even so the Gihon Hunt, like Abu Hussein in the old days, did not understand. Then it reached them through the Press that they habitually flogged to death good revenue-paying cultivators who neglected to stop earths ; but that the few, the very few, who did not die under hippo-hide whips soaked in copperas, walked about on their gangrenous anklebones, and were known in derision as the Mudir's Cranes. The charges were vouched for in the House of Commons by a Mr. Lethabie Groombride, who had formed a Committee, and was disseminating literature. The Province groaned ; the Inspector—now an Inspector of Inspectors—whistled. He had forgotten the gentleman who sputtered in people's faces.

' He shouldn't have looked so like Beagle-boy ! ' was his sole defence when he met the Governor at breakfast on the steamer after a meet.

' You shouldn't have joked with an animal of that class,' said Peter the Governor. ' Look what Farag has brought me ! '

It was a pamphlet, signed on behalf of a Committee by a lady secretary, but composed by some person who thoroughly understood the language of the Province. After telling the tale of the beatings, it recommended all the beaten to institute criminal proceedings against their Governor, and, as soon as might be, to rise against English oppression and tyranny. Such documents were new in Ethiopia in those days.

The Inspector read the last half-page. 'But —but,' he stammered, 'this is impossible. White men don't write this sort of stuff.'

'Don't they, just?' said the Governor. 'They get made Cabinet Ministers for doing it too. I went home last year. *I* know.'

'It'll blow over,' said the Inspector weakly.

'Not it. Groombride is coming down here to investigate the matter in a few days.'

'For himself?'

'The Imperial Government's behind him. Perhaps you'd like to look at my orders.' The Governor laid down an uncoded cable. The whip-lash to it ran: 'You will afford Mr. Groombride every facility for his inquiry, and will be held responsible that no obstacles are put in his way to the fullest possible examination of any witnesses which he may consider necessary. He will be accompanied by his own interpreter, who must not be tampered with.'

'That's to me—Governor of the Province!' said Peter the Governor.

'It seems about enough,' the Inspector answered.

Farag, kennel-huntsman, entered the saloon, as was his privilege.

'My uncle, who was beaten by the Father of Waterwheels, would approach, O Excellency,' he said, 'and there are also others on the bank.'

'Admit,' said the Governor.

There tramped aboard Sheikhs and villagers to the number of seventeen. In each man's hand was a copy of the pamphlet; in each man's eye terror and uneasiness of the sort that Governors spend and are spent to clear away. Farag's uncle, now Sheikh of the village, spoke: 'It is written in this book, O Excellency, that the beatings whereby we hold our lands are all valueless. It is written that every man who received such a beating from the Father of Waterwheels who slew the Emirs should instantly begin a lawsuit, because the title to his land is not valid.'

'It is so written. We do not wish lawsuits. We wish to hold our land as it was given to us after the Days of the Oppression,' they cried all together.

The Governor glanced at the Inspector. This was serious. To cast doubt on the ownership of land means, in Ethiopia, the letting in of waters, and the getting out of troops.

'Your titles are good,' said the Governor. The Inspector confirmed with a nod.

'Then what is the meaning of these writings which come from down the river where the Judges are?' Farag's uncle waved his copy. 'By whose order are we ordered to slay *you*, O Excellency Our Governor?'

' It is not written that you are to slay me.'

' Not in those very words, but if we leave an earth unstopped, it is the same as though we wished to save Abu Hussein from the hounds. These writings say: " Abolish your rulers." How can we abolish except we kill? We hear rumours of one who comes from down the river soon to lead us to kill.'

' Fools ! ' said the Governor. ' Your titles are good. This is madness ! '

' It is so written,' they answered like a pack.

' Listen,' said the Inspector smoothly. ' I know who caused the writings to be written and sent. He is a man of a blue-mottled jowl, in aspect like Bigglebai who ate unclean matters. He will come up the river and will give tongue about the beatings.'

' Will he impeach our land-titles? An evil day for him ! '

' Go slow, Baker,' the Governor whispered. ' They'll kill him if they get scared about their land.'

' I tell a parable.' The Inspector lit a cigarette. ' Declare which of you took to walk the children of Milkmaid? '

' Melik-meid First or Second? ' said Farag quickly.

' The second—the one which was lamed by the thorn.'

' No—no. Melik-meid the Second strained her shoulder leaping my water-channel,' a Sheikh cried. ' Melik-meid the First was lamed by the thorns on the day when Our Excellency fell thrice.'

' True—true. The second Melik-meid's mate was Malvolio, the pied hound,' said the Inspector.

' I had two of the second Melik-meid's pups,' said Farag's uncle. ' They died of the madness in their ninth month.'

' And how did they do before they died?' said the Inspector.

' They ran about in the sun and slavered at the mouth till they died.'

' Wherefore?'

' God knows. He sent the madness. It was no fault of mine.'

' Thine own mouth hath answered thee,' the Inspector laughed. ' It is with men as it is with dogs. God afflicts some with a madness. It is no fault of ours if such men run about in the sun and froth at the mouth. The man who is coming will emit spray from his mouth in speaking, and will always edge and push in towards his hearers. When ye see and hear him ye will understand that he is afflicted of God: being mad. He is in God's Hand.'

' But our titles! Are our titles to our lands good?' the crowd repeated.

' Your titles are in my hands—they are good,' said the Governor.

' And he who wrote the writings is an afflicted of God?' said Farag's uncle.

' The Inspector hath said it,' cried the Governor. ' Ye will see when the man comes. O Sheikhs and men, have we ridden together and walked puppies together, and bought and sold

R

barley for the horses, that, after these years, we should run riot on the scent of a madman—an afflicted of God?'

'But the Hunt pays us to kill mad jackals,' said Farag's uncle. 'And he who questions my titles to my land——'

'Aahh! 'Ware riot!' The Governor's hunting-crop cracked like a three-pounder. 'By Allah,' he thundered, 'if the afflicted of God come to any harm at your hands, I myself will shoot every hound and every puppy, and the Hunt shall ride no more. On your heads be it. Go in peace, and tell the others.'

'The Hunt shall ride no more?' said Farag's uncle. 'Then how can the land be governed? No—no, O Excellency Our Governor, we will not harm a hair on the head of the afflicted of God. He shall be to us as is Abu Hussein's wife in her breeding season.'

When they were gone the Governor mopped his forehead.

'We must put a few soldiers in every village this Groombride visits, Baker. Tell 'em to keep out of sight, and have an eye on the villagers. He's trying 'em rather high.'

'O Excellency,' said the smooth voice of Farag, laying *The Field* and *Country Life* square on the table, 'is the afflicted of God who resembles Bigglebai one with the man whom the Inspector met in the great house in England, and to whom he told the tale of the Mudir's Cranes?'

'The same man, Farag,' said the Inspector.

'I have often heard the Inspector tell the tale

to Our Excellency at feeding-time in the kennels ; but since I am in the Government service I have never told it to my people.   May I loose that tale among the villages ? '

The Governor nodded.   ' No harm,' said he.

.   .   .   .   .

The details of Mr. Groombride's arrival, with his interpreter, who, he proposed, should eat with him at the Governor's table, his allocution to the Governor on the New Movement and the sins of Imperialism, I purposely omit.   At three in the afternoon Mr. Groombride said : ' I will go out now and address your victims in this village.'

' Won't you find it rather hot ? ' said the Governor.   ' They generally take a nap till sunset at this time of year.'

Mr. Groombride's large, loose lips set.   ' *That*,' he replied pointedly, ' would be enough to decide me.   I fear you have not quite mastered your instructions.   May I ask you to send for my interpreter ?   I hope he has not been tampered with by your subordinates.'

He was a yellowish boy called Abdul, who had well eaten and drunk with Farag.   The Inspector, by the way, was not present at the meal.

' At whatever risk, I shall go unattended,' said Mr. Groombride.   ' Your presence would cow them from giving evidence.   Abdul, my good friend, would you very kindly open the umbrella ? '

He passed up the gang-plank to the village, and with no more prelude than a Salvation Army

picket in a Portsmouth slum, cried: ' Oh, my
brothers ! '

He did not guess how his path had been prepared. The village was widely awake. Farag, in
loose, flowing garments, quite unlike a kennel-
huntsman's khaki and puttees, leaned against the
wall of his uncle's house. ' Come and see the
afflicted of God,' he cried musically, ' whose face,
indeed, resembles that of Bigglebai.'

The village came, and decided that on the
whole Farag was right.

' I can't quite catch what they are saying,' said
Mr. Groombride.

' They saying they very much pleased to see
you, sar,' Abdul interpreted.

' Then I do think they might have sent a
deputation to the steamer; but I suppose they
were frightened of the officials. Tell them not
to be frightened, Abdul.'

' He says you are not to be frightened,' Abdul
explained. A child here sputtered with laughter.
' Refrain from mirth,' Farag cried. ' The afflicted
of God is the guest of The Excellency Our
Governor. We are responsible for every hair of
his head.'

' He has none,' a voice spoke. ' He has the
white and the shining mange.'

' Now tell them what I have come for, Abdul,
and please keep the umbrella well up. I think I
shall reserve myself for my little vernacular speech
at the end.'

' Approach ! Look ! Listen !' Abdul chanted.
' The afflicted of God will now make sport. Pres-

ently he will speak in your tongue, and will consume you with mirth. I have been his servant for three weeks. I will tell you about his undergarments and his perfumes for his head.'

He told them at length.

'And didst thou take any of his perfume bottles?' said Farag at the end.

'I am his servant. I took two,' Abdul replied.

'Ask him,' said Farag's uncle, 'what he knows about our land-titles. Ye young men are all alike.' He waved a pamphlet. Mr. Groombride smiled to see how the seed sown in London had borne fruit by Gihon. Lo, all the seniors held copies of the pamphlet!

'He knows less than a buffalo. He told me on the steamer that he was driven out of his own land by Demah-Kerazi, which is a devil inhabiting crowds and assemblies,' said Abdul.

'Allah between us and Evil!' a woman cackled from the darkness of a hut. 'Come in, children, he may have the Evil Eye.'

'No, my aunt,' said Farag. 'No afflicted of God has an evil eye. Wait till ye hear his mirth-provoking speech which he will deliver. I have heard it twice from Abdul.'

'They seem very quick to grasp the point. How far have you got, Abdul?'

'All about the beatings, sar. They are highly interested.'

'Don't forget about the local self-government, and please hold the umbrella over me. It is hopeless to destroy unless one first builds up.'

'He may not have the Evil Eye,' Farag's

uncle grunted, 'but his devil led him too certainly to question my land-title. Ask him whether he still doubts my land-title?'

'Or mine, or mine?' cried the elders.

'What odds? He is an afflicted of God,' Farag called. 'Remember the tale I told you.'

'Yes, but he is an Englishman, and doubtless of influence, or Our Excellency would not entertain him. Bid that down-country jackass ask him.'

'Sar,' said Abdul, 'these people much fearing they may be turned out of their land in consequence of your remarks. Therefore they ask you to make promise no bad consequences following your visit.'

Mr. Groombride held his breath and turned purple. Then he stamped his foot.

'Tell them,' he cried, 'that if a hair of any one of their heads is touched by any official on any account whatever, all England shall ring with it. Good God! What callous oppression! The dark places of the earth are full of cruelty.' He wiped his face, and throwing out his arms cried: 'Tell them, oh! tell the poor serfs not to be afraid of me. Tell them I come to redress their wrongs—not, Heaven knows, to add to their burden.'

The long-drawn gurgle of the practised public speaker pleased them much.

'That is how the new water-tap runs out in the kennel,' said Farag. 'The Excellency Our Governor entertains him that he may make sport. Make him say the mirth-moving speech.'

'What did he say about my land-titles?'
Farag's uncle was not to be turned.

'He says,' Farag interpreted, 'that he desires
nothing better than that you should live on your
lands in peace. He talks as though he believed
himself to be Governor.'

'Well. We here are all witnesses to what
he has said. Now go forward with the sport.'
Farag's uncle smoothed his garments. 'How
diversely hath Allah made His creatures! On
one He bestows strength to slay Emirs. Another
He causes to go mad and wander in the sun, like
the afflicted sons of Melik-meid.'

'Yes, and to emit spray from the mouth, as
the Inspector told us. All will happen as the
Inspector foretold,' said Farag. 'I have never
yet seen the Inspector thrown out during any run.'

'I think,'—Abdul plucked at Mr. Groombride's sleeves,—'I think perhaps it is better now,
sar, if you give your fine little native speech.
They not understanding English, but much
pleased at your condescensions.'

'Condescensions?' Mr. Groombride spun
round. 'If they only knew how I felt towards
them in my heart! If I could express a tithe of
my feelings! I must stay here and learn the
language. Hold up the umbrella, Abdul! I
think my little speech will show them I know
something of their *vie intime*.'

It was a short, simple, carefully-learned address,
and the accent, supervised by Abdul on the
steamer, allowed the hearers to guess its meaning,
which was a request to see one of the Mudir's

Cranes; since the desire of the speaker's life, the object to which he would consecrate his days, was to improve the condition of the Mudir's Cranes. But first he must behold them with his own eyes. Would, then, his brethren, whom he loved, show him a Mudir's Crane whom he desired to love?

Once, twice, and again in his peroration he repeated his demand, using always—that they might see he was acquainted with their local argot—using always, I say, the word which the Inspector had given him in England long ago—the short adhesive word which, by itself, surprises even unblushing Ethiopia.

There are limits to the sublime politeness of an ancient people. A bulky, blue-chinned man in white clothes, his name red-lettered across his lower shirt-front, spluttering from under a green-lined umbrella almost tearful appeals to be introduced to the Unintroducible; naming loudly the Unnameable; dancing, as it seemed, in perverse joy at mere mention of the Unmentionable— found those limits. There was a moment's hush, and then such mirth as Gihon through his centuries had never heard—a roar like to the roar of his own cataracts in flood. Children cast themselves on the ground, and rolled back and forth cheering and whooping; strong men, their faces hidden in their clothes, swayed in silence, till the agony became insupportable, and they threw up their heads and bayed at the sun; women, mothers and virgins, shrilled shriek upon mounting shriek, and slapped their thighs as it might have been the roll of musketry. When they tried to draw breath, some half-strangled voice would quack out the word, and the riot began afresh. Last to fall was the city-trained Abdul. He held on to the edge of apoplexy, then collapsed, throwing the umbrella from him.

Mr. Groombride should not be judged too harshly. Exercise and strong emotion under a hot sun, the shock of public ingratitude, for the moment ruffled his spirit. He furled the umbrella, and with it beat the prostrate Abdul, crying that he had been betrayed.

In which posture the Inspector, on horseback, followed by the Governor, suddenly found him.

.   .   .   .   .

'That's all very well,' said the Inspector, when he had taken Abdul's dramatically dying depositions on the steamer, 'but you can't hammer a native merely because he laughs at you. I see nothing for it but for the law to take its course.'

'You might reduce the charge to—er—tampering with an interpreter,' said the Governor. Mr. Groombride was too far gone to be comforted.

'It's the publicity that I fear,' he wailed. 'Is there no possible means of hushing up the affair? You don't know what a question—a single question in the House means to a man in my position —the ruin of my political career, I assure you.'

'I shouldn't have imagined it,' said the Governor thoughtfully.

'And, though perhaps I ought not to say it, I am not without honour in my own country—or influence. A word in season, as you know, Your Excellency. It might carry an official far.'

The Governor shuddered.

' Yes, *that* had to come too,' he said to himself. ' Well, look here. If I tell this man of yours to withdraw the charge against you, you can go to Gehenna for aught I care. The only condition I make is, that if you write—I suppose that's part of your business—about your travels, you don't praise *me* ! '

So far Mr. Groombride has loyally adhered to this understanding.

GALLIO'S SONG

ALL day long to the judgment-seat
    The crazed Provincials drew—
All day long at their ruler's feet
    Howled for the blood of the Jew.
Insurrection with one accord
    Banded itself and woke,
And Paul was about to open his mouth
    When Achaia's Deputy spoke :—

' Whether the God descend from above
    Or the Man ascend upon high,
Whether this maker of tents be Jove
    Or a younger deity—
I will be no judge between your gods
    And your godless bickerings.
Lictor, drive them hence with rods—
    I care for none of these things !

' Were it a question of lawful due
    Or Caesar's rule denied,
Reason would I should bear with you
    And order it well to be tried ;
But this is a question of words and names.
    I know the strife it brings.
I will not pass upon any your claims.
    I care for none of these things !

' One thing only I see most clear,
    As I pray you also see.
Claudius Caesar hath set me here
    Rome's Deputy to be.
It is Her peace that ye go to break—
    Not mine, nor any king's.
But, touching your clamour of " Conscience' sake,"
    I care for none of these things.

' Whether ye rise for the sake of a creed,
    Or riot in hope of spoil,

Equally will I punish the deed,
  Equally check the broil ;
Nowise permitting injustice at all,
  From whatever doctrine it springs—
But—whether ye follow Priapus or Paul,
  I care for none of these things ! '

The House Surgeon

The House Surgeon

ON an evening after Easter Day, I sat at a table in a homeward-bound steamer's smoking-room, where half-a-dozen of us told ghost stories. As our party broke up, a man, playing Patience in the next alcove, said to me: ' I didn't quite catch the end of that last story about the Curse on the family's first-born.'

' It turned out to be drains,' I explained. ' As soon as new ones were put into the house the Curse was lifted, I believe. I never knew the people myself.'

' Ah! I've had *my* drains up twice; I'm on gravel too.'

' You don't mean to say you've a ghost in your house? Why didn't you join our party?'

' Any more orders, gentlemen, before the bar closes?' the steward interrupted.

' Sit down again and have one with me,' said the Patience player. ' No, it isn't a ghost. Our trouble is more depression than anything else.'

' How interesting! Then it's nothing any one can see?'

' It's—it's nothing worse than a little depression. And the odd part is that there hasn't been

265

a death in the house since it was built—in 1863. The lawyer said so. That decided me—my good lady, rather—and he made me pay an extra thousand for it.'

'How curious! Unusual, too!' I said.

'Yes, ain't it? It was built for three sisters— Moultrie was the name—three old maids. They all lived together; the eldest owned it. I bought it from her lawyer a few years ago, and if I've spent a pound on the place first and last, I must have spent five thousand. Electric light, new servants' wing, garden—all that sort of thing. A man and his family ought to be happy after so much expense, ain't it?' He looked at me through the bottom of his glass.

'Does it affect your family much?'

'My good lady—she's a Greek by the way— and myself are middle-aged. We can bear up against depression; but it's hard on my little girl. I say little; but she's twenty. We send her visiting to escape it. She almost lived at hotels and hydros last year, but that isn't pleasant for her. She used to be a canary—a perfect canary —always singing. You ought to hear her. She doesn't sing now. That sort of thing's unwholesome for the young, ain't it?'

'Can't you get rid of the place?' I suggested.

'Not except at a sacrifice, and we are fond of it. Just suits us three. We'd love it if we were allowed.'

'What do you mean by not being allowed?'

'I mean because of the depression. It spoils everything.'

' What's it like exactly? '

' I couldn't very well explain. It must be seen to be appreciated, as the auctioneers say. Now, I was much impressed by the story you were telling just now.'

' It wasn't true,' I said.

' My tale is true. If you would do me the pleasure to come down and spend a night at my little place, you'd learn more than you would if I talked till morning. Very likely 'twouldn't touch your good self at all. You might be—immune, ain't it? On the other hand, if this influenza-influence *does* happen to affect you, why, I think it will be an experience.'

While he talked he gave me his card, and I read his name was L. Maxwell M'Leod, Esq., of Holmescroft. A City address was tucked away in a corner.

' My business,' he added, ' used to be furs. If you are interested in furs—I've given thirty years of my life to 'em.'

' You're very kind,' I murmured.

' Far from it, I assure you. I can meet you next Saturday afternoon anywhere in London you choose to name, and I'll be only too happy to motor you down. It ought to be a delightful run at this time of year—the rhododendrons will be out. I mean it. You don't know how truly I mean it. Very probably—it won't affect you at all. And—I think I may say I have the finest collection of narwhal tusks in the world. All the best skins and horns have to go through London, and L. Maxwell M'Leod, he knows where they come from, and where they go to. That's his business.'

For the rest of the voyage up-Channel Mr. M'Leod talked to me of the assembling, preparation, and sale of the rarer furs; and told me things about the manufacture of fur-lined coats which quite shocked me. Somehow or other, when we landed on Wednesday, I found myself pledged to spend that week-end with him at Holmescroft.

On Saturday he met me with a well-groomed motor, and ran me out in an hour and a half to an exclusive residential district of dustless roads and elegantly designed country villas, each standing in from three to five acres of perfectly appointed land. He told me land was selling at eight hundred pounds the acre, and the new golf links, whose Queen Anne pavilion we passed, had cost nearly twenty-four thousand pounds to create.

Holmescroft was a large, two-storied, low, creeper-covered residence. A veranda at the south side gave on to a garden and two tennis courts, separated by a tasteful iron fence from a most park-like meadow of five or six acres, where two Jersey cows grazed. Tea was ready in the shade of a promising copper beech, and I could see groups on the lawn of young men and maidens appropriately clothed, playing lawn tennis in the sunshine.

' A pretty scene, ain't it?' said Mr. M'Leod. ' My good lady's sitting under the tree, and that's my little girl in pink on the far court. But I'll take you to your room, and you can see 'em all later.'

He led me through a wide parquet-floored hall furnished in pale lemon, with huge cloisonné vases, an ebonised and gold grand piano, and banks of pot flowers in Benares brass bowls, up a pale oak staircase to a spacious landing, where there was a green velvet settee trimmed with silver. The blinds were down, and the light lay in parallel lines on the floors.

He showed me my room, saying cheerfully: ' You may be a little tired.   One often is without knowing it after a run through traffic.   Don't come down till you feel quite restored.   We shall all be in the garden.'

My room was rather close, and smelt of perfumed soap.   I threw up the window at once, but it opened so close to the floor and worked so clumsily that I came within an ace of pitching out, where I should certainly have ruined a rather lopsided laburnum below.   As I set about washing off the journey's dust, I began to feel a little tired. But, I reflected, I had not come down here in this weather and among these new surroundings to be depressed, so I began to whistle.

And it was just then that I was aware of a little grey shadow, as it might have been a snowflake seen against the light, floating at an immense distance in the background of my brain.   It annoyed me, and I shook my head to get rid of it. Then my brain telegraphed that it was the forerunner of a swift-striding gloom which there was yet time to escape if I would force my thoughts away from it, as a man leaping for life forces his body forward and away from the fall of a wall.

But the gloom overtook me before I could take in the meaning of the message. I moved toward the bed, every nerve already aching with the fore-knowledge of the pain that was to be dealt it, and sat down, while my amazed and angry soul dropped, gulf by gulf, into that Horror of great darkness which is spoken of in the Bible, and which, as auctioneers say, must be experienced to be appreciated.

Despair upon despair, misery upon misery, fear after fear, each causing their distinct and separate woe, packed in upon me for an unrecorded length of time, until at last they blurred together, and I heard a click in my brain like the click in the ear when one descends in a diving-bell, and I knew that the pressures were equalised within and with-out, and that, for the moment, the worst was at an end. But I knew also that at any moment the darkness might come down anew; and while I dwelt on this speculation precisely as a man torments a raging tooth with his tongue, it ebbed away into the little grey shadow on the brain of its first coming, and once more I heard my brain, which knew what would recur, telegraph to every quarter for help, release, or diversion.

The door opened, and M'Leod reappeared. I thanked him politely, saying I was charmed with my room, anxious to meet Mrs. M'Leod, much refreshed with my wash, and so on and so forth. Beyond a little stickiness at the corners of my mouth, it seemed to me that I was managing my words admirably, the while that I myself cowered at the bottom of unclimbable pits.

M'Leod laid his hand on my shoulder, and said:
' You've got it now already, ain't it? '

' Yes,' I answered, ' it's making me sick! '

' It will pass off when you come outside. I give
you my word it will then pass off. Come! '

I shambled out behind him, and wiped my
forehead in the hall.

' You mustn't mind,' he said. ' I expect the
run tired you. My good lady is sitting there under
the copper beech.'

She was a fat woman in an apricot-coloured
gown, with a heavily powdered face, against which
her black long-lashed eyes showed like currants
in dough. I was introduced to many fine ladies
and gentlemen of those parts. Magnificently
appointed landaus and covered motors swept in
and out of the drive, and the air was gay with the
merry outcries of the tennis-players.

As twilight drew on they all went away, and I
was left alone with Mr. and Mrs. M'Leod, while
tall men-servants and maid-servants took away the
tennis and tea things. Miss M'Leod had walked
a little down the drive with a light-haired young
man, who apparently knew everything about every
South American railway stock. He had told me
at tea that these were the days of financial
specialisation.

' I think it went off beautifully, my dear,'
said Mr. M'Leod to his wife; and to me:
' You feel all right now, ain't it? Of course
you do.'

Mrs. M'Leod surged across the gravel. Her
husband skipped nimbly before her into the south

veranda, turned a switch, and all Holmescroft was flooded with light.

' You can do that from your room also,' he said as they went in. ' There is something in money, ain't it? '

Miss M'Leod came up behind me in the dusk. ' We have not yet been introduced,' she said, ' but I suppose you are staying the night? '

' Your father was kind enough to ask me,' I replied.

She nodded. ' Yes, *I* know ; and you know too, don't you? I saw your face when you came to shake hands with mamma. You felt the depression very soon? It is simply frightful in that bedroom sometimes. What do you think it is— bewitchment? In Greece, where I was a little girl, it might have been ; but not in England, do you think? Or *do* you? '

' I don't know what to think,' I replied. ' I never felt anything like it. Does it happen often? '

' Yes, sometimes. It comes and goes.'

' Pleasant ! ' I said, as we walked up and down the gravel at the lawn edge. ' What has been your experience of it? '

' That is difficult to say, but—sometimes that —that depression is like as it were '—she gesticu- lated in most un-English fashion—' a light. Yes, like a light turned into a room—only a light of blackness, do you understand?—into a happy room. For sometimes we are so happy, all we three,—so *very* happy. Then this blackness, it is turned on us just like—ah, I know what I mean now—like the head-lamp of a motor, and we are eclip-sed. And there is another thing——'

The dressing-gong roared, and we entered the over-lighted hall. My dressing was a brisk athletic performance, varied with outbursts of song—careful attention paid to articulation and expression. But nothing happened. As I hurried downstairs, I thanked Heaven that nothing had happened.

Dinner was served breakfast-fashion; the dishes were placed on the sideboard over heaters, and we helped ourselves.

' We always do this when we are alone, so we talk better,' said Mr. M'Leod.

' And we are always alone,' said the daughter.

' Cheer up, Thea. It will all come right,' he insisted.

' No, papa.' She shook her dark head. ' Nothing is right while *it* comes.'

' It is nothing that we ourselves have ever done in our lives—that I will swear to you,' said Mrs. M'Leod suddenly. ' And we have changed our servants several times. So we know it is not *them*.'

' Never mind. Let us enjoy ourselves while we can,' said Mr. M'Leod, opening the champagne.

But we did not enjoy ourselves. The talk failed. There were long silences.

' I beg your pardon,' I said, for I thought some one at my elbow was about to speak.

' Ah! That is the other thing!' said Miss M'Leod. Her mother groaned.

We were silent again, and, in a few seconds it must have been, a live grief beyond words—not ghostly dread or horror, but aching, helpless grief —overwhelmed us, each, I felt, according to his or her nature, and held steady like the beam of a burning-glass. Behind that pain I was conscious there was a desire on somebody's part to explain something on which some tremendously important issue hung.

Meantime I rolled bread pills and remembered my sins; M'Leod considered his own reflection in a spoon; his wife seemed to be praying, and the girl fidgeted desperately with hands and feet till the darkness passed on—as though the malignant rays of a burning-glass had been shifted from us.

'There,' said Miss M'Leod, half rising. 'Now you see what makes a happy home. Oh, sell it— sell it, father mine, and let us go away!'

'But I've spent thousands on it. You shall go to Harrogate next week, Thea dear.'

'I'm only just back from hotels. I am *so* tired of packing.'

'Cheer up, Thea. It is over. You know it does not often come here twice in the same night. I think we shall dare now to be comfortable.'

He lifted a dish-cover, and helped his wife and daughter. His face was lined and fallen like an old man's after a debauch, but his hand did not shake, and his voice was clear. As he worked to restore us by speech and action, he reminded me of a grey-muzzled collie herding demoralised sheep.

After dinner we sat round the dining-room fire—the drawing-room might have been under the Shadow for aught we knew—talking with the intimacy of gipsies by the wayside, or of wounded comparing notes after a skirmish. By eleven o'clock the three between them had given me every name and detail they could recall that in any way bore on the house, and what they knew of its history.

We went to bed in a fortifying blaze of electric light. My one fear was that the blasting gust of depression would return—the surest way, of course, to bring it. I lay awake till dawn, breathing quickly and sweating lightly, beneath what De Quincey inadequately describes as 'the oppression of inexpiable guilt.' Now as soon as the lovely day was broken, I fell into the most terrible of all dreams—that joyous one in which all past evil has not only been wiped out of our lives, but has never been committed; and in the very bliss of our assured innocence, before our loves shriek and change countenance, we wake to the day we have earned.

It was a coolish morning, but we preferred to breakfast in the south veranda. The forenoon we spent in the garden, pretending to play games that come out of boxes, such as croquet and clock-golf. But most of the time we drew together and talked. The young man who knew all about South American railways took Miss M'Leod for a walk in the afternoon, and at five M'Leod thoughtfully whirled us all up to dine in town.

' Now, don't say you will tell the Psychological

Society, and that you will come again,' said Miss M'Leod, as we parted. 'Because I know you will not.'

'You should not say that,' said her mother. 'You should say, "Good-bye, Mr. Perseus. Come again."'

'Not him!' the girl cried. 'He has seen the Medusa's head!'

Looking at myself in the restaurant's mirrors, it seemed to me that I had not much benefited by my week-end. Next morning I wrote out all my Holmescroft notes at fullest length, in the hope that by so doing I could put it all behind me. But the experience worked on my mind, as they say certain imperfectly understood rays work on the body.

I am less calculated to make a Sherlock Holmes than any man I know, for I lack both method and patience, yet the idea of following up the trouble to its source fascinated me. I had no theory to go on, except a vague idea that I had come between two poles of a discharge, and had taken a shock meant for some one else. This was followed by a feeling of intense irritation. I waited cautiously on myself, expecting to be overtaken by horror of the supernatural, but my self persisted in being humanly indignant, exactly as though it had been the victim of a practical joke. It was in great pains and upheavals—that I felt in every fibre—but its dominant idea, to put it coarsely, was to get back a bit of its own. By this I knew that I might go forward if I could find the way.

After a few days it occurred to me to go to the office of Mr. J. M. M. Baxter—the solicitor who had sold Holmescroft to M'Leod. I explained I had some notion of buying the place. Would he act for me in the matter?

Mr. Baxter, a large, greyish, throaty-voiced man, showed no enthusiasm. 'I sold it to Mr. M'Leod,' he said. 'It 'ud scarcely do for me to start on the running-down tack now. But I can recommend——'

'I know he's asking an awful price,' I interrupted, 'and atop of it he wants an extra thousand for what he calls your clean bill of health.'

Mr. Baxter sat up in his chair. I had all his attention.

'Your guarantee with the house. Don't you remember it?'

'Yes, yes. That no death had taken place in the house since it was built. I remember perfectly.'

He did not gulp as untrained men do when they lie, but his jaws moved stickily, and his eyes, turning towards the deed-boxes on the wall, dulled. I counted seconds, one, two, three—one, two, three—up to ten. A man, I knew, can live through ages of mental depression in that time.

'I remember perfectly.' His mouth opened a little as though it had tasted old bitterness.

'Of course *that* sort of thing doesn't appeal to me,' I went on. '*I* don't expect to buy a house free from death.'

'Certainly not. No one does. But it was Mr. M'Leod's fancy—his wife's rather, I believe;

and since we could meet it—it was my duty to
my clients—at whatever cost to my own feelings—
to make him pay.'

' That's really why I came to you. I understood from him you knew the place well.'

' Oh yes. Always did. It originally belonged
to some connections of mine.'

' The Misses Moultrie, I suppose. How interesting! They must have loved the place
before the country round about was built up.'

' They were very fond of it indeed.'

' I don't wonder. So restful and sunny. I
don't see how they could have brought themselves to part with it.'

Now it is one of the most constant peculiarities
of the English that in polite conversation—and I
had striven to be polite—no one ever does or sells
anything for mere money's sake.

' Miss Agnes — the youngest — fell ill ' (he
spaced his words a little), ' and, as they were very
much attached to each other, that broke up the
home.'

' Naturally. I fancied it must have been something of that kind. One doesn't associate the
Staffordshire Moultries ' (my Demon of Irre-
sponsibility at that instant created 'em) ' with—
with being hard up.'

' I don't know whether we're related to them,'
he answered importantly. ' We may be, for our
branch of the family comes from the Midlands.'

I give this talk at length, because I am so proud
of my first attempt at detective work. When I
left him, twenty minutes later, with instructions

to move against the owner of Holmescroft with a
view to purchase, I was more bewildered than any
Doctor Watson at the opening of a story.

Why should a middle-aged solicitor turn
plover's-egg colour and drop his jaw when reminded of so innocent and festal a matter as
that no death had ever occurred in a house that
he had sold? If I knew my English vocabulary
at all, the tone in which he said the youngest sister
' fell ill ' meant that she had gone out of her mind.
That might explain his change of countenance,
and it was just possible that her demented influence still hung about Holmescroft. But the
rest was beyond me.

I was relieved when I reached M'Leod's City
office, and could tell him what I had done—not
what I thought.

M'Leod was quite willing to enter into the
game of the pretended purchase, but did not see
how it would help if I knew Baxter.

' He's the only living soul I can get at who was
connected with Holmescroft,' I said.

' Ah! Living soul is good,' said M'Leod.
' At any rate our little girl will be pleased that you
are still interested in us. Won't you come down
some day this week? '

' How is it there now? ' I asked.

He screwed up his face. ' Simply frightful! '
he said. ' Thea is at Droitwich.'

' I should like it immensely, but I must cultivate Baxter for the present. You'll be sure and
keep him busy your end, won't you? '

He looked at me with quiet contempt. ' Do

not be afraid. I shall be a good Jew. I shall be my own solicitor.'

Before a fortnight was over, Baxter admitted ruefully that M'Leod was better than most firms in the business. We buyers were coy, argumentative, shocked at the price of Holmescroft, inquisitive, and cold by turns, but Mr. M'Leod the seller easily met and surpassed us; and Mr. Baxter entered every letter, telegram, and consultation at the proper rates in a cinematograph-film of a bill. At the end of a month he said it looked as though M'Leod, thanks to him, were really going to listen to reason. I was some pounds out of pocket, but I had learned something of Mr. Baxter on the human side. I deserved it. Never in my life have I worked to conciliate, amuse, and flatter a human being as I worked over my solicitor.

It appeared that he golfed. Therefore, I was an enthusiastic beginner, anxious to learn. Twice I invaded his office with a bag (M'Leod lent it) full of the spelicans needed in this detestable game, and a vocabulary to match. The third time the ice broke, and Mr. Baxter took me to his links, quite ten miles off, where in a maze of tramway-lines, railroads, and nursery-maids, we skelped our divoted way round nine holes like barges plunging through head seas. He played vilely and had never expected to meet any one worse; but as he realised my form, I think he began to like me, for he took me in hand by the two hours together. After a fortnight he could give me no more than a stroke a hole, and when, with this allowance, I once managed to beat him by one, he was honestly glad, and assured me that I should be a golfer if I stuck to it. I was sticking to it for my own ends, but now and again my conscience pricked me; for the man was a nice man. Between games he supplied me with odd pieces of evidence, such as that he had known the Moultries all his life, being their cousin, and that Miss Mary, the eldest, was an unforgiving woman who would never let by-gones be. I naturally wondered what she might have against him; and somehow connected him unfavourably with mad Agnes.

'People ought to forgive and forget,' he volunteered one day between rounds. 'Specially where, in the nature of things, they can't be sure of their deductions. Don't you think so?'

'It all depends on the nature of the evidence on which one forms one's judgment,' I answered.

'Nonsense!' he cried. 'I'm lawyer enough to know that there's nothing in the world so mis-leading as circumstantial evidence. Never was.'

'Why? Have you ever seen men hanged on it?'

'Hanged? People have been supposed to be eternally lost on it.' His face turned grey again. 'I don't know how it is with you, but my con-solation is that God must know. He *must*! Things that seem on the face of 'em like murder, or say suicide, may appear different to God. Heh?'

'That's what the murderer and the suicide can always hope—I suppose.'

'I have expressed myself clumsily as usual.

The facts as God knows 'em—may *be* different—
even after the most clinching evidence. I've
always said that—both as a lawyer and a man, but
some people won't—I don't want to judge 'em—
we'll say they can't—believe it; whereas *I* say
there's always a working chance—a certainty—
that the worst hasn't happened.' He stopped
and cleared his throat. ' Now, let's come on !
This time next week I shall be taking my holiday.'

' What links ? ' I asked carelessly, while twins
in a perambulator got out of our line of fire.

' A potty little nine-hole affair at a Hydro in
the Midlands. My cousins stay there. Always
will. Not but what the fourth and the seventh
holes take some doing. You could manage it,
though,' he said encouragingly. ' You're doing
much better. It's only your approach-shots that
are weak.'

' You're right. I can't approach for nuts ! I
shall go to pieces while you're away—with no one
to coach me,' I said mournfully.

' I haven't taught you anything,' he said,
delighted with the compliment.

' I owe all I've learned to you, anyhow. When
will you come back ? '

' Look here,' he began. ' I don't know your
engagements, but I've no one to play with at
Burry Mills. Never have. Why couldn't you
take a few days off and join me there ? I warn
you it will be rather dull. It's a throat and gout
place—baths, massage, electricity, and so forth.
But the fourth and the seventh holes really take
some doing.'

'I'm for the game,' I answered valiantly, Heaven well knowing that I hated every stroke and word of it.

'That's the proper spirit. As their lawyer I must ask you not to say anything to my cousins about Holmescroft. It upsets 'em. Always did. But speaking as man to man, it would be very pleasant for me if you could see your way to——'

I saw it as soon as decency permitted, and thanked him sincerely. According to my now well-developed theory he had certainly misappropriated his aged cousins' monies under power of attorney, and had probably driven poor Agnes Moultrie out of her wits, but I wished that he was not so gentle, and good-tempered, and innocent-eyed.

Before I joined him at Burry Mills Hydro, I spent a night at Holmescroft. Miss M'Leod had returned from her Hydro, and first we made very merry on the open lawn in the sunshine over the manners and customs of the English resorting to such places. She knew dozens of Hydros, and warned me how to behave in them, while Mr. and Mrs. M'Leod stood aside and adored her.

'Ah! That's the way she always comes back to us,' he said. 'Pity it wears off so soon, ain't it? You ought to hear her sing " With mirth, thou pretty bird." '

We had the house to face through the evening, and there we neither laughed nor sang. The gloom fell on us as we entered, and did not shift till ten o'clock, when we crawled out, as it were, from beneath it.

'It has been bad this summer,' said Mrs. M'Leod in a whisper after we realised that we were freed. 'Sometimes I think the house will get up and cry out—it is so bad.'

'How?'

'Have you forgotten what comes after the depression?'

So then we waited about the small fire, and the dead air in the room presently filled and pressed down upon us with the sensation (but words are useless here) as though some dumb and bound power were striving against gag and bond to deliver its soul of an articulate word. It passed in a few minutes, and I fell to thinking about Mr. Baxter's conscience and Agnes Moultrie, gone mad in the well-lit bedroom that waited me. These reflections secured me a night during which I rediscovered how, from purely mental causes, a man can be physically sick. But the sickness was bliss compared with my dreams when the birds waked. On my departure, M'Leod gave me a beautiful narwhal's horn much as a nurse gives a child sweets for being brave at a dentist's.

'There's no duplicate of it in the world,' he said, 'else it would have come to old Max M'Leod,' and he tucked it into the motor. Miss M'Leod on the far side of the car whispered, 'Have you found out anything, Mr. Perseus?'

I shook my head.

'Then I shall be chained to my rock all my life,' she went on. 'Only don't tell papa.'

I supposed she was thinking of the young gentleman who specialised in South American

rails, for I noticed a ring on the third finger of her
left hand.

I went straight from that house to Burry
Mills Hydro, keen for the first time in my life on
playing golf, which is guaranteed to occupy the
mind.   Baxter had taken me a room communi-
cating with his own, and after lunch introduced
me to a tall, horse-headed elderly lady of decided
manners, whom a white-haired maid pushed along
in a bath-chair through the park-like grounds of
the Hydro.   She was Miss Mary Moultrie, and
she coughed and cleared her throat just like
Baxter.   She suffered—she told me it was the
Moultrie caste-mark—from some obscure form of
chronic bronchitis, complicated with spasm of the
glottis; and, in a dead flat voice, with a sunken
eye that looked and saw not, told me what washes,
gargles, pastilles, and inhalations she had proved
most beneficial.   From her I was passed on to
her younger sister, Miss Elizabeth, a small and
withered thing with twitching lips, victim, she
told me, to very much the same sort of throat,
but secretly devoted to another set of medicines.
When she went away with Baxter and the bath-
chair, I fell across a Major of the Indian Army
with gout in his glassy eyes, and a stomach which
he had taken all round the Continent.   He laid
everything before me; and him I escaped only
to be confided in by a matron with a tendency
to follicular tonsillitis and eczema.   Baxter waited
hand and foot on his cousins till five o'clock, trying, as I saw, to atone for his treatment of the dead
sister.   Miss Mary ordered him about like a dog.

' I warned you it would be dull,' he said when
we met in the smoking-room.

' It's tremendously interesting,' I said. ' But
how about a look round the links? '

' Unluckily damp always affects my eldest
cousin. I've got to buy her a new bronchitis-
kettle. Arthurs broke her old one yesterday.'

We slipped out to the chemist's shop in the
town, and he bought a large glittering tin thing
whose workings he explained.

' I'm used to this sort of work. I come up
here pretty often,' he said. ' I've the family
throat too.'

' You're a good man,' I said. ' A very good
man.'

He turned toward me in the evening light
among the beeches, and his face was changed to
what it might have been a generation before.

' You see,' he said huskily, ' there was the
youngest—Agnes. Before she fell ill, you know.
But she didn't like leaving her sisters. Never
would.' He hurried on with his odd-shaped load
and left me among the ruins of my black theories.
The man with that face had done Agnes Moultrie
no wrong.

.   .   .   .   .

We never played our game. I was waked
between two and three in the morning from my
hygienic bed by Baxter in an ulster over orange-
and-white pyjamas, which I should never have
suspected from his character.

' My cousin has had some sort of a seizure,'
he said. ' Will you come? I don't want to wake

the doctor. Don't want to make a scandal. Quick!'

So I came quickly, and, led by the white-haired Arthurs in a jacket and petticoat, entered a double-bedded room reeking with steam and Friar's Balsam. The electrics were all on. Miss Mary—I knew her by her height—was at the open window, wrestling with Miss Elizabeth, who gripped her round the knees. Her hand was at her throat, which was streaked with blood.

'She's done it. She's done it too!' Miss Elizabeth panted. 'Hold her! Help me!'

'Oh, I say! Women don't cut their throats,' Baxter whispered.

'My God! Has she cut her throat?' the maid cried, and with no warning rolled over in a faint. Baxter pushed her under the wash-basins, and leaped to hold the gaunt woman who crowed and whistled as she struggled towards the window. He took her by the shoulder, and she struck out wildly.

'All right! She's only cut her hand,' he said. 'Wet towel—quick!'

While I got that he pushed her backward. Her strength seemed almost as great as his. I swabbed at her throat when I could, and found no mark; then helped him to control her a little. Miss Elizabeth leaped back to bed, wailing like a child.

'Tie up her hand somehow,' said Baxter. 'Don't let it drip about the place. She'—he stepped on broken glass in his slippers—'she must have smashed a pane.'

Miss Mary lurched towards the open window again, dropped on her knees, her head on the sill, and lay quiet, surrendering the cut hand to me.

'What did she do?' Baxter turned towards Miss Elizabeth in the far bed.

'She was going to throw herself out of the window,' was the answer. 'I stopped her, and sent Arthurs for you. Oh, we can never hold up our heads again!'

Miss Mary writhed and fought for breath. Baxter found a shawl which he threw over her shoulders.

'Nonsense!' said he. 'That isn't like Mary'; but his face worked when he said it.

'You wouldn't believe about Aggie, John. Perhaps you will now!' said Miss Elizabeth. 'I *saw* her do it, and she's cut her throat too!'

'She hasn't,' I said. 'It's only her hand.'

Miss Mary suddenly broke from us with an indescribable grunt, flew, rather than ran, to her sister's bed, and there shook her as one furious schoolgirl would shake another.

'No such thing,' she croaked. 'How dare you think so, you wicked little fool?'

'Get into bed, Mary,' said Baxter. 'You'll catch a chill.'

She obeyed, but sat up with the grey shawl round her lean shoulders, glaring at her sister. 'I'm better now,' she crowed. 'Arthurs let me sit out too long. Where's Arthurs? The kettle.'

'Never mind Arthurs,' said Baxter. '*You* get the kettle.' I hastened to bring it from the side-table. 'Now, Mary, as God sees you, tell me what you've done.'

His lips were dry, and he could not moisten them with his tongue.

Miss Mary applied herself to the mouth of the kettle, and between indraws of steam said: 'The spasm came on just now, while I was asleep. I was nearly choking to death. So I went to the window. I've done it often before, without waking any one. Bessie's such an old maid about draughts! I tell you I was choking to death. I couldn't manage the catch, and I nearly fell out. That window opens too low. I cut my hand trying to save myself. Who has tied it up in this filthy handkerchief? I wish you had had my throat, Bessie. I never was nearer dying!' She scowled on us all impartially, while her sister sobbed.

From the bottom of the bed we heard a quivering voice: 'Is she dead? Have they took her away? Oh, I never could bear the sight o' blood!'

'Arthurs,' said Miss Mary, 'you are an hireling. Go away!'

It is my belief that Arthurs crawled out on all fours, but I was busy picking up broken glass from the carpet.

Then Baxter, seated by the side of the bed, began to cross-examine in a voice I scarcely recognised. No one could for an instant have doubted the genuine rage of Miss Mary against her sister, her cousin, or her maid; and that the doctor should have been called in—for she did me the honour of calling me doctor—was the last drop. She was choking with her throat;

had rushed to the window for air; had nearly pitched out, and in catching at the window-bars had cut her hand. Over and over she made this clear to the intent Baxter. Then she turned on her sister and tongue-lashed her savagely.

'You mustn't blame me,' Miss Bessie faltered at last. ' You know what we think of night and day.'

' I'm coming to that,' said Baxter. ' Listen to me. What *you* did, Mary, misled four people into thinking you—you meant to do away with yourself.'

' Isn't one suicide in the family enough? Oh, God, help and pity us! You *couldn't* have believed that! ' she cried.

' The evidence was complete. Now, don't you think,'—Baxter's finger wagged under her nose—' *can't* you think that poor Aggie did the same thing at Holmescroft when she fell out of the window? '

' She had the same throat,' said Miss Elizabeth. ' Exactly the same symptoms. Don't you remember, Mary? '

' Which was her bedroom? ' I asked of Baxter in an undertone.

' Over the south veranda, looking on to the tennis lawn.'

' I nearly fell out of that very window when I was at Holmescroft—opening it to get some air. The sill doesn't come much above your knees,' I said.

' You hear that, Mary? Mary, do you hear what this gentleman says? Won't you believe that what nearly happened to you must have happened to poor Aggie that night? For God's sake—for her sake—Mary, *won't* you believe?'

There was a long silence while the steam-kettle puffed.

'If I could have proof—if I could have proof,' said she, and broke into most horrible tears.

Baxter motioned to me, and I crept away to my room, and lay awake till morning, thinking more specially of the dumb Thing at Holmescroft which wished to explain itself. I hated Miss Mary as perfectly as though I had known her for twenty years, but I felt that, alive or dead, I should not like her to condemn me.

Yet at mid-day, when I saw Miss Mary in her bath-chair, Arthurs behind and Baxter and Miss Elizabeth on either side, in the park-like grounds of the Hydro, I found it difficult to arrange my words.

'Now that you know all about it,' said Baxter aside, after the first strangeness of our meeting was over, 'it's only fair to tell you that my poor cousin did not die *in* Holmescroft at all. She was dead when they found her under the window in the morning. Just dead.'

'Under that laburnum outside the window?' I asked, for I suddenly remembered the crooked evil thing.

'Exactly. She broke the tree in falling. But no death has ever taken place *in* the house, so far as we were concerned. You can make yourself quite easy on that point. Mr. M'Leod's extra thousand for what you called the " clean bill of health " was something towards my cousins' estate when we sold. It was my duty as their lawyer to get it for them—at any cost to my own feelings.'

I know better than to argue when the English talk about their duty. So I agreed with my solicitor.

'Their sister's death must have been a great blow to your cousins,' I went on. The bath-chair was behind me.

'Unspeakable,' Baxter whispered. 'They brooded on it day and night. No wonder. If their theory of poor Aggie making away with herself was correct, she was eternally lost!'

'Do you believe that she made away with herself?'

'No, thank God! Never have! And after what happened to Mary last night, I see perfectly what happened to poor Aggie. She had the family throat too. By the way, Mary thinks you are a doctor. Otherwise she wouldn't like your having been in her room.'

'Very good. Is she convinced now about her sister's death?'

'She'd give anything to be able to believe it, but she's a hard woman, and brooding along certain lines makes one groovy. I have sometimes been afraid for her reason—on the religious side, don't you know. Elizabeth doesn't matter. Brain of a hen. Always had.'

Here Arthurs summoned me to the bath-chair, and the ravaged face, beneath its knitted Shetland wool hood, of Miss Mary Moultrie.

'I need not remind you, I hope, of the seal of

secrecy—absolute secrecy—in your profession,'
she began.   ' Thanks to my cousin's and my
sister's stupidity, you have found out——' She
blew her nose.

' Please don't excite her, sir,' said Arthurs at
the back.

' But, my dear Miss Moultrie, I only know
what I've seen, of course, but it seems to me that
what you thought was a tragedy in your sister's
case, turns out, on your own evidence, so to speak,
to have been an accident—a dreadfully sad one—
but absolutely an accident.'

' Do you believe that too? ' she cried. ' Or are
you only saying it to comfort me? '

' I believe it from the bottom of my heart.
Come down to Holmescroft for an hour—for half
an hour—and satisfy yourself.'

' Of what? You don't understand. I see the
house every day—every night. I am always there
in spirit—waking or sleeping. I couldn't face it
in reality.'

' But you must,' I said. ' If you go there in
the spirit the greater need for you to go there in
the flesh. Go to your sister's room once more,
and see the window—I nearly fell out of it myself.
It's—it's awfully low and dangerous. That would
convince you,' I pleaded.

' Yet Aggie had slept in that room for years,'
she interrupted.

' You've slept in your room here for a long
time, haven't you? But you nearly fell out of
the window when you were choking.'

' That is true. That is one thing true,' she

nodded. 'And I might have been killed as—perhaps—Aggie was killed.'

'In that case your own sister and cousin and maid would have said you had committed suicide, Miss Moultrie. Come down to Holmescroft, and go over the place just once.'

'You are lying,' she said quite quietly. 'You don't want me to come down to see a window. It is something else. I warn you we are Evangelicals. We don't believe in prayers for the dead. "As the tree falls——" '

'Yes. I daresay. But you persist in thinking that your sister committed suicide——'

'No! No! I have always prayed that I might have misjudged her.'

Arthurs at the bath-chair spoke up: 'Oh, Miss Mary! you *would* 'ave it from the first that poor Miss Aggie 'ad made away with herself; an', of course, Miss Bessie took the notion from you. Only Master—Mister John stood out, and —and I'd 'ave taken my Bible oath *you* was making away with yourself last night.'

Miss Mary leaned towards me, one finger on my sleeve.

'If going to Holmescroft kills me,' she said, ' you will have the murder of a fellow-creature on your conscience for all eternity.'

'I'll risk it,' I answered. Remembering what torment the mere reflection of her torments had cast on Holmescroft, and remembering, above all, the dumb Thing that filled the house with its desire to speak, I felt that there might be worse things.

Baxter was amazed at the proposed visit, but at a nod from that terrible woman went off to make arrangements. Then I sent a telegram to M'Leod bidding him and his vacate Holmescroft for that afternoon. Miss Mary should be alone with her dead, as I had been alone.

I expected untold trouble in transporting her, but to do her justice, her promise given for the journey, she underwent it without murmur, spasm, or unnecessary word. Miss Bessie, pressed in a corner by the window, wept behind her veil, and from time to time tried to take hold of her sister's hand. Baxter wrapped himself in his newly-found happiness as selfishly as a bridegroom, for he sat still and smiled.

' So long as I know that Aggie didn't make away with herself,' he explained, ' I tell you frankly I don't care what happened. She's as hard as a rock—Mary. Always was. *She* won't die.'

We led her out on to the platform like a blind woman, and so got her into the fly. The half-hour crawl to Holmescroft was the most racking experience of the day. M'Leod had obeyed my instructions. There was no one visible in the house or the gardens ; and the front door stood open.

Miss Mary rose from beside her sister, stepped forth first, and entered the hall.

' Come, Bessie,' she cried.

' I daren't. Oh, I daren't.'

' Come ! ' Her voice had altered. I felt Baxter start. ' There's nothing to be afraid of.'

' Good heavens ! ' said Baxter. ' She's running
up the stairs.   We'd better follow.'

' Let's wait below.   She's going to the room.'

We heard the door of the bedroom I knew
open and shut, and we waited in the lemon-
coloured hall, heavy with the scent of flowers.

' I've never been into it since it was sold,'
Baxter sighed.   ' What a lovely restful place it
is !   Poor Aggie used to arrange the flowers.'

'Restful?' I began, but stopped of a sudden, for
I felt all over my bruised soul that Baxter was
speaking truth.   It was a light, spacious, airy
house, full of the sense of well-being and peace—
above all things, of peace.   I ventured into the
dining-room where the thoughtful M'Leods had
left a small fire.   There was no terror there present
or lurking ; and in the drawing-room, which for
good reasons we had never cared to enter, the sun
and the peace and the scent of the flowers worked
together as is fit in an inhabited house.   When I
returned to the hall, Baxter was sweetly asleep on
a couch, looking most unlike a middle-aged
solicitor who had spent a broken night with an
exacting cousin.

There was ample time for me to review it all—
to felicitate myself upon my magnificent acumen
(barring some errors about Baxter as a thief and
possibly a murderer), before the door above
opened, and Baxter, evidently a light sleeper,
sprang awake.

' I've had a heavenly little nap,' he said,
rubbing his eyes with the backs of his hands like
a child.   ' Good Lord !   That's not *their* step ! '

But it was. I had never before been privileged to see the Shadow turned backward on the dial— the years ripped bodily off poor human shoulders —old sunken eyes filled and alight—harsh lips moistened and human.

'John,' Miss Mary called, 'I know now. Aggie didn't do it!' and 'She didn't do it!' echoed Miss Bessie, and giggled.

'I did not think it wrong to say a prayer,' Miss Mary continued. 'Not for her soul, but for our peace. Then I was convinced.'

'Then we got conviction,' the younger sister piped.

'We've misjudged poor Aggie, John. But I feel she knows now. Wherever she is, she knows that we know she is guiltless.'

'Yes, she knows. I felt it too,' said Miss Elizabeth.

'I never doubted,' said John Baxter, whose face was beautiful at that hour. 'Not from the first. Never have!'

'You never offered me proof, John. Now, thank God, it will not be the same any more. I can think henceforward of Aggie without sorrow.' She tripped, absolutely tripped, across the hall. 'What ideas these Jews have of arranging furniture!' She spied me behind a big cloisonné vase.

'I've seen the window,' she said remotely. 'You took a great risk in advising me to undertake such a journey. However, as it turns out . . . I forgive you, and I pray you may never know what mental anguish means! Bessie!

Look at this peculiar piano! Do you suppose,
Doctor, these people would offer one tea? I miss
mine.'

'I will go and see,' I said, and explored
M'Leod's new-built servants' wing. It was in
the servants' hall that I unearthed the M'Leod
family bursting with anxiety.

'Tea for three, quick,' I said. 'If you ask
me any questions now, I shall have a fit!' So
Mrs. M'Leod got it, and I was butler, amid
murmured apologies from Baxter, still smiling
and self-absorbed, and the cold disapproval of
Miss Mary, who thought the pattern of the china
vulgar. However, she ate well, and even asked
me whether I would not like a cup of tea for
myself.

They went away in the twilight—the twilight
that I had once feared. They were going to an
hotel in London to rest after the fatigues of the
day, and as their fly turned down the drive, I
capered on the doorstep, with the all-darkened
house behind me.

Then I heard the uncertain feet of the M'Leods,
and bade them not to turn on the lights, but to feel
—to feel what I had done; for the Shadow was
gone, with the dumb desire in the air. They drew
short, but afterwards deeper, breaths, like bathers
entering chill water, separated one from the
other, moved about the hall, tiptoed upstairs, raced
down, and then Miss M'Leod, and I believe her
mother, though she denies this, embraced me. I
know M'Leod did.

It was a disgraceful evening. To say we rioted

through the house is to put it mildly. We played a sort of Blind Man's Buff along the darkest passages, in the unlighted drawing-room, and the little dining-room, calling cheerily to each other after each exploration that here, and here, and here, the trouble had removed itself. We came up to *the* bedroom—mine for the night again— and sat, the women on the bed, and we men on chairs, drinking in blessed draughts of peace and comfort and cleanliness of soul, while I told them my tale in full, and received fresh praise, thanks, and blessing.

When the servants, returned from their day's outing, gave us a supper of cold fried fish, M'Leod had sense enough to open no wine. We had been practically drunk since nightfall, and grew incoherent on water and milk.

'I like that Baxter,' said M'Leod. 'He's a sharp man. The death wasn't *in* the house, but he ran it pretty close, ain't it?'

'And the joke of it is that he supposes I want to buy the place from you,' I said. 'Are you selling?'

'Not for twice what I paid for it—now,' said M'Leod. 'I'll keep you in furs all your life; but not our Holmescroft.'

'No—never our Holmescroft,' said Miss M'Leod. 'We'll ask *him* here on Tuesday, mamma.' They squeezed each other's hands.

'Now tell me,' said Mrs. M'Leod—' that tall one I saw out of the scullery window—did *she* tell you she was always here in the spirit? I hate her. She made all this trouble. It was *not* her house after she had sold it. What do you think?'

'I suppose,' I answered, 'she brooded over what she believed was her sister's suicide night and day—she confessed she did—and her thoughts being concentrated on this place, they felt like a —like a burning-glass.'

'Burning-glass is good,' said M'Leod.

'I said it was like a light of blackness turned on us,' cried the girl, twiddling her ring. 'That must have been when the tall one thought worst about her sister and the house.'

'Ah, the poor Aggie!' said Mrs. M'Leod. 'The poor Aggie, trying to tell every one it was not so! No wonder we felt Something wished to say Something. Thea, Max, do you remember that night——'

'We need not remember any more,' M'Leod interrupted. 'It is not our trouble. They have told each other now.'

'Do you think, then,' said Miss M'Leod, 'that those two, the living ones, were actually told something—upstairs—in your—in the room?'

'I can't say. At any rate they were made happy, and they ate a big tea afterwards. As your father says, it is not our trouble any longer— thank God!'

'Amen!' said M'Leod. 'Now, Thea, let us have some music after all these months. "With mirth, thou pretty bird," ain't it? You ought to hear that.'

And in the half-lighted hall, Thea sang an old English song that I had never heard before :—

With mirth, thou pretty bird, rejoice
   Thy Maker's praise enhancèd ;
Lift up thy shrill and pleasant voice,
   Thy God is high advancèd !
Thy food before He did provide,
And gives it in a fitting side,
   Wherewith be thou sufficèd !
Why shouldst thou now unpleasant be,
   Thy wrath against God venting,
That He a little bird made thee,
   Thy silly head tormenting,
Because He made thee not a man ?
Oh, Peace ! He hath well thought thereon,
   Therewith be thou sufficèd !

THE RABBI'S SONG

I f Thought can reach to Heaven,
    On Heaven let it dwell,
For fear that Thought be given
    Like power to reach to Hell.
For fear the desolation
    And darkness of thy mind
Perplex an habitation
    Which thou hast left behind.

Let nothing linger after—
    No whimpering ghost remain,
In wall, or beam, or rafter,
    Of any hate or pain.
Cleanse and call home thy spirit,
    Deny her leave to cast,
On aught thy heirs inherit,
    The shadow of her past.

For think, in all thy sadness,
    What road our grief may take ;
Whose brain reflect our madness,
    Or whom our terrors shake.
For think, lest any languish
    By cause of thy distress—
The arrows of our anguish
    Fly farther than we guess.

Our lives, our tears, as water,
    Are poured upon the ground.
God giveth no man quarter,
    Yet God a means hath found—
Though Faith and Hope have vanished,
    And even Love grows dim,—
A means whereby His banished
    Be not expelled from Him !